THE BEAUTY
OF TIME

EXECUTIVE EDITOR
Suzanne Tise-Isoré
Collection Style & Design

EDITORIAL COORDINATION AT
THE FONDATION DE LA HAUTE HORLOGERIE
Grégory Gardinetti

EDITORIAL COORDINATION
Lara Lo Calzo

GRAPHIC DESIGN
Bernard Lagacé
Lysandre Le Cléac'h

TRANSLATED FROM THE FRENCH BY
Alexandra Keens

CAPTIONS TRANSLATED FROM THE FRENCH BY
Lucian Comoy for Language Consulting Congressi, Milan

PROOFREADING
Lindsay Porter

PRODUCTION
Élodie Conjat

COLOR SEPARATION
Les Artisans du Regard, Paris

PRINTED BY
Musumeci, Italy
Certified FSC®

Simultaneously published in French as *La Beauté du Temps*.

Flammarion S.A.
87, quai Panhard et Levassor
75647 Paris Cedex 13
editions.flammarion.com
styleetdesign-flammarion.com

Fondation de la Haute Horlogerie
4, rue André-De-Garrini
1217 Meyrin, Switzerland
hautehorlogerie.org

18 19 20 3 2 1
ISBN: 978-2-08-020341-0
Edition Number: L.01EBTN000810
Legal Deposit: 01/2018

Printed on certified-FSC® paper in Italy

PAGE 3
PIERRE-EDME BABEL (1720–1775),
Clock, 1700s. Rothschild collection.
Musée du Louvre, Paris.

ACKNOWLEDGMENTS

The authors would like to thank the Fondation de la Haute Horlogerie
and all the people who offered their support and fruitful exchanges over
the preparation and publication of this volume. Moreover, François Chaille
expresses his gratitude to the art critic Philippe Piguet.

For their generous support, the publisher especially thanks Jean-Michel
Piguet of Musée international d'horlogerie at La Chaux-de-Fonds, Monika
Winkler of Beyer Zurich Clock and Watch Museum, the antiques dealer
Richard Redding, Eveline Meeuwse Hoster, Alexandre de Vogüé of the
château de Vaux-Le-Vicomte, and château de Villette, together with
the following maisons: Alfred Dunhill, Audemars Piguet, Beat Haldimann,
Blancpain, Bovet 1822, Breguet, Cartier, Chaumet, Chopard, Girard-
Perregaux, Greubel Forsey, Hermès, Hublot, HYT, Jaeger-LeCoultre, Jaquet
Droz, Lip, Longines, Marc Newson Ltd., MB&F, Omega, Officine Panerai,
Parmigiani Fleurier, Piaget, Richard Mille, Roger Dubuis, Swatch, TAG Heuer,
Ulysse Nardin, Vacheron Constantin, and Van Cleef & Arpels.

THE BEAUTY
OF TIME

FRANÇOIS CHAILLE
DOMINIQUE FLÉCHON

Foreword
FRANCO COLOGNI

Flammarion

FHH
FONDATION HAUTE HORLOGERIE
FOUNDATION HIGH HOROLOGY

CONTENTS

FACING PAGE
GERRIT DOU (1613–1675),
*Still Life with Candle and Pocket
Watch*, c. 1660. Staatliche
Kunstsammlungen, Dresden.

A JOURNEY THROUGH THE ART OF TIME

In the cloister of the Piccolo Teatro of Milan is a sundial bearing an inscription that has always captured my imagination: *Horas non numero nisi serenas*: "I count only the sunny (bright, serene) hours"—in other words, the happy hours. Writing the foreword to this book, which takes us on a journey through the beauty of time, brought back this memory and also provided me with a link between two of my greatest interests: watchmaking and theater. What these two arts have in common is that in order to work well, actions in time must be precisely sequenced and measured, and effectively staged. And, in both cases, technical prowess is not enough to rouse emotions; it takes wonderment, sentiment, pathos—in a word, beauty.

In my university days I used go to the Piccolo Teatro, which was the first theater of our time to bring the art to a wider public, and I would read that inscription on the sundial and think of the great performers whose skills offered their spectators some truly happy moments, and of the characters on stage who could inject poetry into every story. Today, sixty years later, thinking about that all too rare magic, it occurs to me that the masterpieces presented in this book enchant us in similar ways, as they turn minutes into memories and emotions.

I have never been an actor nor a master watchmaker. But I have endeavored to bring to these two worlds, which are very much part of who I am, the modest talent that I have cultivated over the years in France and in Italy, that of a stage director. Each time I have penned a good scenario for the world of fine and beautiful watchmaking, I have sought to capture its most significant, yet seemingly unconnected traits (artistic skill and mechanical skill; uniqueness and business; desire and the balance sheet), so as to create a naturally resonant dialogue between the two; in many cases, I have been able, like a good theater troupe director, to come up with something that works, and that gave me great joy.

I usually like to think up different ways to explore the story of watchmaking—one that my friend Dominique Fléchon has told in the pages of the brilliant repository of culture that is *The Beauty of Time*. But also the story of all the beautiful, admirable, and astonishing things that are reflected in watchmaking, and which we relate in this book. This was a choice that, I hope, will be of interest to readers, at a time when beauty is perhaps the last quality to show us truth—albeit in ways that are often difficult to understand.

The Greek poet Yannis Ritsos said that behind every beautiful thing is a multitude of stitches, patiently sewn with an invisible needle. In the world of watchmaking, these stitches transcend facts and dates, tying up with the inventions, special commissions, ambitions, and dreams of people who have a passion not so much for time itself, but for the beauty of time. It is precisely these evanescent stitches, retraced with a novelist's skill by François Chaille, in the light of the history, the art, and the events of humanity, that we have chosen to relate here, through the miracles of the human heart and mind, rather than studying their development through time. The list of contents alone suggests a plot worthy of a novel: the Time of the Cathedrals, the Time of the Renaissance, the Time of the Seventeenth Century—or "Grand Siècle" in France—the Time of the Enlightenment. Not their dates, but their spirit; a portrayal not of stages but rather of trends, focusing on long periods of time, on cultural factors, and on changing concepts of the "magical," through those precious and rare objects that are timepieces. In a word, a journey through the art of time, whose protagonists are magnificent masterpieces of "timeless" beauty.

In so doing, François Chaille and the authoritative historian Dominique Fléchon together composed these pages that are valuable both as a narrative and a scholarly study.

Lavish illustrations also provide the transitions between ideas and periods; not only of clocks and watches, but also of art works symbolizing a moment in time, an era, or a whole world. Because we believe that beauty in its most elegant tradition is never spontaneously revealed, but rather reserves its finest face for the beholder wise enough to seek it out, we have also selected images with hidden messages to discover and decipher. Readers will encounter timepieces that do not occupy center stage but that ideally complement it. In his fresco in the Salone dei Cinquecento in Florence's Palazzo Vecchio, Vasari wrote on a flag "*Cerca Trova*" (Seek and you shall find), fueling speculation as to the presence beneath his work of traces of Leonardo da Vinci's encaustic painting *The Battle of Anghiari*.

In conclusion, the beauty of time is beauty that moves in the right direction, toward precision, progress, perfection. It is also the beauty of poetry, of lightness, of sophisticated technology, of material and forms that the human mind, hand, and heart have never ceased to improve and enhance; creating in the process an envelope for that most precious element, time, in its dimension most authentically close to our own condition, to be "a little lower than the angels": beauty.

This beauty arises from surprise, from curiosity, from a perception of truth; and it springs also from the magic of a timepiece: because our eyes are designed to wonder at things, and our heart is made to turn this wonderment into memories that become stories, emotions, and impressions that are not fleeting but that give us confidence to move onward and upward, and the will to count and remember only the "happy hours". And thus to envisage, thanks to the memories and texts, images and stories told in this book, a future that is more "beautiful."

FRANCO COLOGNI

9

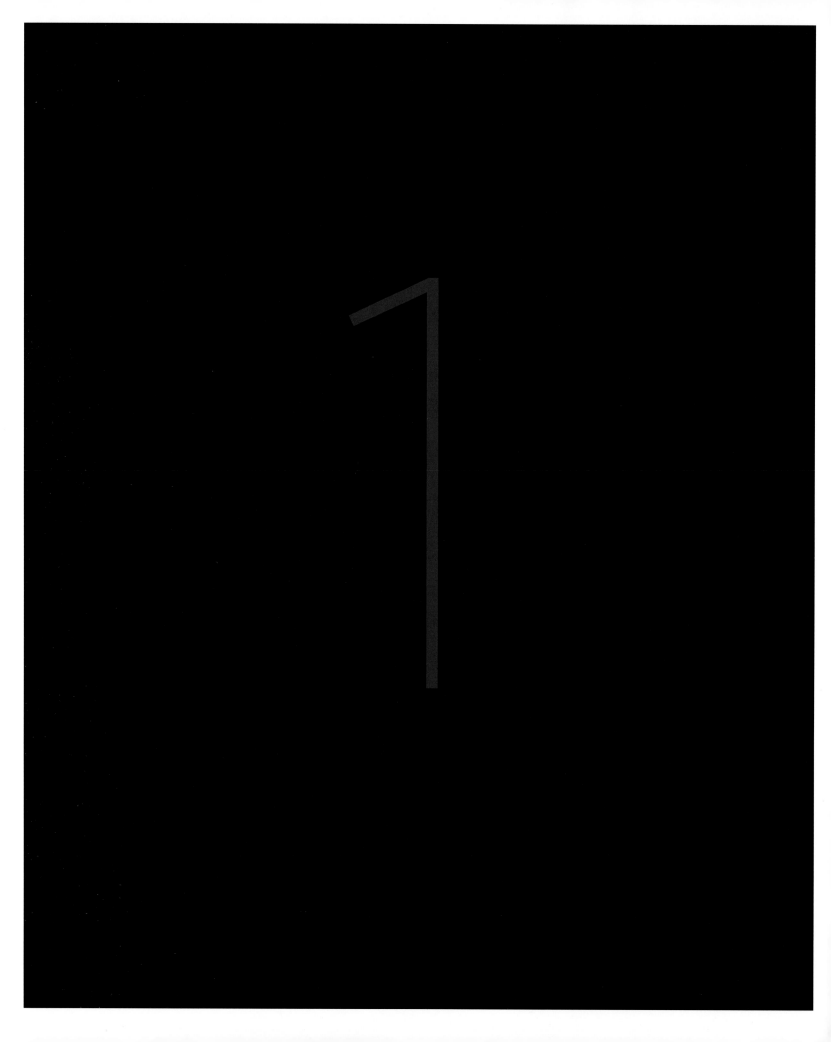

THE TIME OF THE
CATHEDRALS

One day, probably in the very first years of the fourteenth century, although the exact date is not known, a new sound rang out below the immense vaults of Beauvais Cathedral: the music of time. The chiming clock that had just been installed is there to this day, and it is probably the oldest in the world of its kind still in working order. It is located in one of the chapels, the chapel of Saint Teresa, against the wall of the sacristy and the treasury, at the top of a hexagonal stone shaft, 16 ½ ft. (5 m) high, containing its driving weights. At the time of its installation, the clock's dial only had hour hands. Its chime, with a twelve-note keyboard, could play eight different tunes, depending on the feast days through the year. As indicated on its engraved Latin inscription, still visible, the bell that sounded the hour was a gift from one of the cathedral canons, known as Étienne "Musique," no doubt because he was the choirmaster.

It is not known if the clock's wooden casing was decorated at the time. The paintings of angels that still adorn it today date from the fifteenth century, while the indications of the lunar phases were added in the eighteenth century. In all likelihood, the clock's original ornamentation was worthy of the setting in which it was placed. The earliest depictions in art of mechanical clocks, in the fourteenth century, always show them as sculpted or painted. The astronomical clock at the Benedictine abbey of St. Albans, designed by the abbot Richard of Wallingford, appears in an illumination in the *Golden Book of St. Albans*, dating from 1380. But whether it was decorated or not, the beauty of the Beauvais clock doubtless lay entirely in the music

it sounded up to the sky, that magical infinite expanse suggested in the extraordinary height (154 ft./47 m) of the cathedral vaults.

Several dozen of these magnificent religious edifices that were the cathedrals were built between the twelfth and the fourteenth centuries, during the era of Gothic splendor in the West. They were home to the first mechanical clocks, from about 1300, thereby creating an aural environment, together with the liturgical chanting and singing of the choirs, that was evocative of heavenly music. As mechanical devices, these cathedral clocks necessarily marked regular hours. They announced the approximate hour of each mass, and when they had chimes they accompanied the principal religious feast days. But they also met the new needs of city dwellers. The sounding of the hour reminded churchgoers—and other local inhabitants, if the clock was in a bell tower—of their numerous duties and obligations as citizens. The first known example of the secular function of these early cathedral clocks is found in Salisbury, England: a municipal decree of 1306 stipulated that "before the clock of the Cathedral had struck one no person was to purchase or cause to be purchased flesh, fish or other victuals."[1]

However, as pointed out by Roland Recht in his seminal work *Believing and Seeing: The Art of Gothic Cathedrals*,[2] the cathedral was primarily, at the time, a new *image*. Designed and built by technicians and decorated by artists, the cathedral with its polychrome façades—where impressive rituals took place and where worshipers could admire the wonderful sculptures and stained glass all around

FACING PAGE
Located in Beauvais Cathedral, the **CARILLON CLOCK** in the chapel of Saint Teresa is from the early fourteenth century and is one of the oldest of its kind in the world still to be in operation.

PAGES 14–15
JEAN FOUQUET (1420–1481), *The Construction of Solomon's Temple* (1400s). Illustration showing the importance of the construction of cathedrals between the twelfth and fourteenth centuries in the West.

them—was conceived to inspire awe, wonder, and contemplation: it was about "seeing is believing." And nothing could impede this edifying vision, not the comings and goings of the crowds who came there for protection and charity, nor even the permanent clamor of the cries of vendors and noise of animals surrounding the edifice. Since the fourteenth century, a secular town clock would sound the hour in a public space close by—like the one installed in 1315 on the bridge in the city of Caen, in France, which bore this cheerful inscription:

> *Puisqu'ainsi la ville me loge*
> *Sur ce pont pour servir d'auloge,*
> *Je feroy les heures ouïr*
> *Pour le commun peuple esjouir.*
> (Since the city has put me here / On this bridge to serve as a clock / I will sound out the hours / For the common enjoyment of the people.)

Cathedrals became the spiritual hearts of the cities, which were growing rapidly at the time. But a new rationalism had also taken hold of these urban environments. In the twelfth and thirteenth centuries, cities were undergoing a "commercial" revolution, marked by increased exchange and trade, the specialization of labor, growth in land sales, and rural exodus toward urban areas. Because of this, cities were developing an intense cultural life. University-trained men of letters were rediscovering the Classics—Terence, Plato, Seneca, Aristotle, Socrates, Pythagoras—who extoled the greatness of man and his ability to understand the world and its mysteries and beauties. At the same

LEFT
BEAUVAIS CATHEDRAL was one of the boldest constructions of the Middle Ages for the height of its vaults (154 ft./47 m). An astronomical clock with animated figures, made by Lucien Vérité between 1865 and 1868, is just one of the notable works of art it contains.

———

ABOVE
Illustration from the *SPECULUM NATURALE* (Mirror of Nature), a fifteenth-century manuscript, showing Vincent of Beauvais (c. 1190–1264) writing in his private study.

ABOVE AND FACING PAGE
LIMBOURG BROTHERS (fl. 1385–1416),
illuminations from the calendar
of the *Très Riches heures du duc de
Berry* (1411–16), depicting,
from left to right, the months of
July, October, February, and June.
Musée Condé, Chantilly.

PEREUNT ET IMPUTANTUR.

time, people were gaining access to the scientific works of the Arabic scholars, who had in turn been influenced by the Greeks and Persians. In around 1200, one lettered man wrote that it was time to turn away from these "horrible and evil-smelling" times to live "according to reason."

During the construction of the cathedral in which the oldest chiming clock would be installed, a Dominican friar, Vincent of Beauvais, completed, in 1263, the first true encyclopedia. Compiling all of the knowledge acquired in the Middle Ages, it would be the most comprehensive encyclopedia until Diderot and d'Alembert created theirs in the eighteenth century. Commissioned by Louis IX, the *Speculum maius* (Great Mirror), comprised no fewer than eighty books and 9,885 chapters, and was divided into three parts: the *Speculum naturale* (Mirror of Nature), the *Speculum doctrinale* (Mirror of Doctrine), and the *Speculum historiale* (Mirror of History). It was a repository of knowledge of natural history (from light to human anatomy, atmospheric phenomena, and wild and domestic animals), rhetoric, philosophy, and military strategy, as well as "historical acts and deeds" from Genesis to the mid-thirteenth century. Written in Latin, this extensive work was an immense success with men of letters, and was republished many times up until the early seventeenth century.

At the time of the publication of the *Speculum maius*, which coincided with a general effort toward rationalization, some disputed the work: how indeed was it possible to bring together within a single system all "scientific" knowledge and the dogma of the divine Truth? In the late thirteenth century, Aristotle's teachings were condemned by the Church. In around 1300, John Duns Scotus and William of Occam, Franciscans at the university of Oxford, challenged, respectively, man's reason, incapable of proving truths such as divine Providence or oneness, and a science that claimed to classify kinds and species, while disregarding the individual and access to intuitive knowledge.

The power of princes and magistrates weakened the Church and its scholars, however, while promoting philosophical thought that was removed from Church scrutiny, and sciences such as astronomy, optics, and mechanics. In the mid-fourteenth century, Nicholas Oresme, for example, adviser to King Charles V (known as "Charles the Wise") of France, could freely engage in extensive scientific research on economics, mathematics, physics, astronomy, and music.

The period was characterized by a boundless curiosity, an avid desire for knowledge that would provide answers to the great mysteries that were not easy to elucidate: in particular, those of far-off lands. A work on this subject, published in 1298, met with great success: *The Book of the Marvels of the World*, a description of Asia by Marco Polo that was a real "report," and moreover written originally in the vernacular—an Old French dialect with numerous Italianisms. Polo, the son of a Venetian merchant, dictated his account while imprisoned in Genoa, after being captured during a naval battle, to a cellmate who was a writer by profession, Rustichello of Pisa. Added to the wondrous notion of "seeing is believing," Polo now brought the

FACING PAGE
ASTRONOMICAL CLOCK from the fourteenth century in Exeter Cathedral, England, decorated with the Latin motto *Pereunt et Imputantur* ("They [the hours] perish and are reckoned to our account"). Conforming to Ptolemy's principle, the dial depicts the sun and moon revolving around the earth.

———
Anonymous, *SOLOMON OBSERVING THE STARS* (c. 1170–80). Capuchin Bible, collection of the Capuchin monks of rue Saint–Honoré. Bibliothèque Nationale de France, Paris.

ABOVE, LEFT
PORTRAIT OF MARCO POLO (1867),
mosaic in Palazzo Tursi, Genoa.
The son of a Venetian merchant,
Marco Polo (1254–1324) left Venice
for Asia in 1271. Upon his return,
he dictated the account of his
fabulous adventures in his *Book of
the Marvels of the World*.

ABOVE, RIGHT
Boucicaut Master (fl. 1408–1420),
miniature from the *BOOK OF
THE MARVELS OF THE WORLD*,
showing the Mongol emperor
Kublai Khan (1214–1294) proffering
a gold tablet—a sort of passport—
to Marco Polo.

FACING PAGE
The **SLOANE ASTROLABE**
(1290–1300). The oldest and one
of the most enigmatic astrolabes
in the world. Of remarkable quality,
it reveals a sure knowledge of
Arab astronomy and instruments.
British Museum, London.

PAGE 24
Muhammad ibn Ahmad al-Mizzi
(d. 1342), **ASTROLABIC QUADRANT**
(1333–34). Employed at the great
mosque of Damascus, al-Mizzi was
a *muwaqqit*, an astronomer who
determined the exact time of the
five daily Muslim prayers.

PAGE 25
ZAKARIYA AL-QAZWINI (1203–1283),
thirteenth-century gouache depicting
the division of the year shown in
Arabic characters, from *The Wonders of
Creation and Strange Things Existing*.

even more enticing message "If you haven't seen it with your own eyes it is impossible to believe." It was mostly in his capacity as adviser to Kublai Khan, Mongolian emperor of China and founder of the Yuan dynasty, that Polo traveled in Asia, from Japan to Madagascar, Ceylon, India, Indonesia, Vietnam, Burma, Afghanistan, and, naturally, China. Presented as a collection of "marvels," the book contained a mass of information that was not only fascinating at the time, but also accurate, about the geography, customs, economy, techniques, and political life of the Asian peoples. Such as they were described, the fabulous riches of the emperor left the first Venetian readers of the account somewhat skeptical. Yet they were true, like most of the other descriptions.

Half a century later, another explorer, from Ieper, probably called Jan de Langhe but who passed himself off as an English gentleman by the name of Sir John Mandeville, met with even greater success with his *Book of Marvels and Travels*. This travel memoir, describing the author's purported journey from the Holy Land to China, was full of extraordinary legends and extravagant places peopled with animals as monstrous as they were imaginary, headless men, and giants. But the so-called Mandeville incorporated some true facts in his stories, drawn from the accounts of actual travelers, from both recent or ancient times, and from the encyclopedia of Vincent of Beauvais. It was later proven that Mandeville had in fact only visited Egypt. Published in 1356 in the Anglo-Norman language, the book was hugely successful and was translated into a dozen vernacular languages. Its principal merit was to discuss at length the possibility of a round-the-world trip, and as such became one of the works that influenced Christopher Columbus.

In these late Middle Ages, a thirst for knowledge and its corollary, despite the frauds—a rational approach which distanced itself from traditional religious subjects—also emerged in the arts. In France, the foremost writers of the times, such as Christine de Pizan, Charles of Orléans, and François Villon, focused on non-religious subjects: the first with her courtly and almost feminist poems, and her remarkable biography of Charles V;[3] the second with his magnificent love poems and poetry celebrating ordinary pleasures, including his famous poem, *Printemps* (Spring), learnt by schoolchildren to this day (*Le temps a laissié son manteau/De vent, de froidure et de pluye,/Et s'est vestu de brouderie,/De soleil luyant, cler et beau*);[4] and the third, brilliant champion of low-lifes, women, and wine, but who also wrote about the passing of time and of death. In England, Geoffrey Chaucer's bawdy and satirical *Canterbury Tales* were in a similarly non-religious vein. While in Italy, three giants of world literature, Dante, Boccaccio, and Petrarch, who were near contemporaries (the last two were close friends) and all wrote in Tuscan, also illustrated this new trend, although this did not prevent them having a profound faith: Dante with works such as his philosophical *Convivio* (The Banquet), and his account of love, *La Vita Nuova*; Boccaccio with his colorful *Decameron*; and Petrarch with his magnificent and passionate *Canzoniere*.

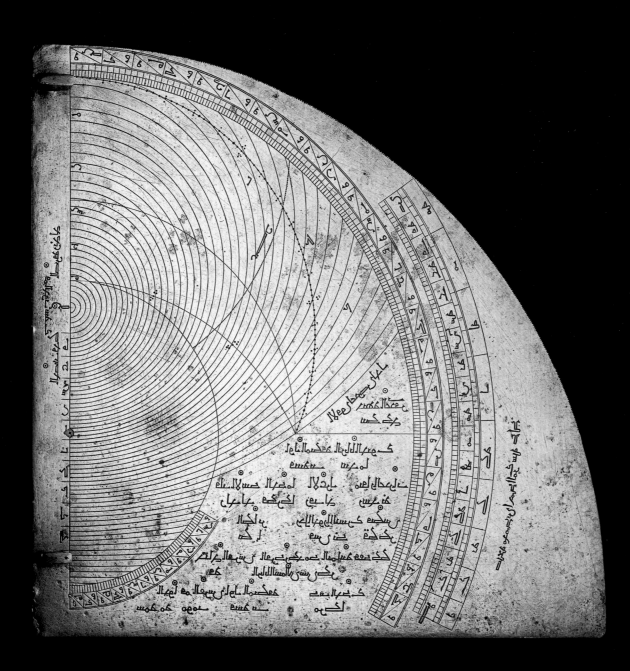

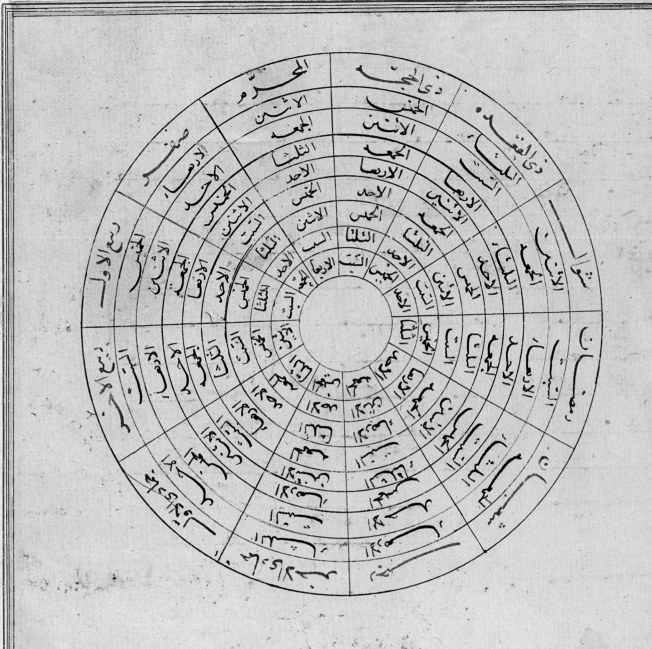

قال جعفر الصادق عليه السلام اذا اشكل عليك اول الشهر رمضان فعد من اول يوم صمته في العام الماضي

فالخامس من اول يوم من شهر رمضان المقبل وامتحن ذلك بعضهم خمسين سنة فكان صحيحا والله اعلم

فصل

في شهور الرومية

وهي مختلفة بالعدد لانهم ارادوا ان يكون شهورهم متكافئة لمسير الشمس وحركات الشمس مختلفة في ارباع السنة فبعضها اكثر اياما من البعض حتى نطقت به الارصاد القديمة والحديثة فلهذا اجلوا بعض الشهور ثلثين وبعضها

All of Petrarch's work, his profound humanism, his effort to conciliate the ancient, pagan, and Christian worlds, heralded the end of the Middle Ages and the beginning of a new age. The work of painters, too, had also begun to reflect this transition, in the fourteenth century: easel painting came back, applying itself initially to portraiture and marking the decline of the purely religious conception of painting in the Middle Ages. The first known easel painting of "modern times" is a portrait of King John II ("the Good") of France (1319–1364) in profile, an oil on wood that is today at the Louvre Museum. Painters now sought to depict people and nature just as they were. In his landscapes, Giotto, who produced countless church frescoes in Italy, moved toward a faithful transcription of reality, using books of sketches made in the midst of nature. But it was mainly in Flanders—whose spectacularly prosperous cities, Bruges, Antwerp, Brussels, Tournai, Ghent, were seeing the earliest forms of a capitalist economy—that a powerful middle class favored painting that would depict and flatter its members. The school of the Flemish Primitives emerged circa 1430, with oil painting, which enabled artists to capture every nuance and produce realistic depictions. Jan Van Eyck and his *Arnolfini Portrait*, Petrus Christus, and Hans Memling, with their numerous splendid portraits executed in Bruges, are among the earliest Netherlandish painters, joined a little later by another genius, Hieronymus Bosch.

It is impossible to cite the artists and various beauties of the late Middle Ages, or to understand the energy and underlying forces of artistic production in the mid-fourteenth century, without mentioning an insidious shadow that hung over the period, which spread and eventually wiped out huge swathes of the population: the plague. The Black Death epidemic that struck Florence in 1348, witnessed by Boccacio, was the driving force, the subject, in part, and the disquieting backdrop of his *Decameron*: "So great and so intense was the cruelty of heaven (and in part, perhaps, the cruelty of men) that, between March and the following July, with the virulence of the plague sickness and with the number of patients not properly cared for, or abandoned in their time of need because the healthy people were too fightened to help, it is believed for certain that more than a hundred thousand human beings perished within the walls of the city of Florence, which, before the arrival of that death-dealing calamity, might not have been thought to house so many people."[5] Among the one-hundred thousand victims of this Florence plage was Laura, the object of Petrarch's love. The plague struck again in the Po Valley thirteen years later, forcing Petrarch to flee to Venice.

The bubonic plague, which originated in China, was brought by the Mongols during their 1346 siege of Kaffa, a Genoese trading post on the banks of the Black Sea (present-day Feodosiya). A truce had enabled the Genoese ships to leave Kaffa—and to take the bacteria to all the ports at which they stopped: Constantinople, Genoa, Messina, and Marseille were hit the following year. In 1348, the plague had spread all around the Mediterranean basin, and then, in just a few months, to all of Europe, North Africa, and the

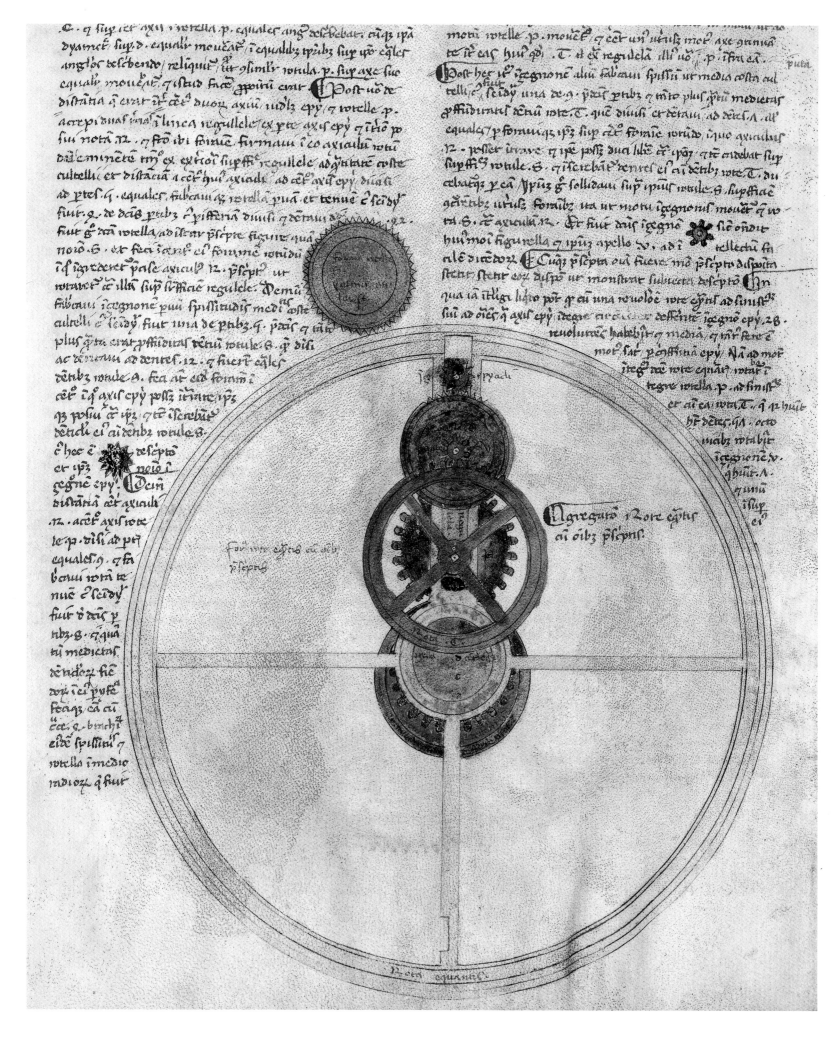

Middle East. It is estimated that between 1347 and 1351, the Black Death wiped out between 30 and 50 percent of the European population, at least twenty-five million people.

In five years, the Great Plague caused many more victims than the other great calamity of the times, the Hundred Years' War, which from 1337 to 1453 opposed England and France. The civil populations were largely spared by this conflict, in which Plantagenet knights fought Valois knights, and even the defeated fighters were often exchanged for a ransom. The plague, however, turned an entire continent into a terrifying kingdom of death, which obsessed everyone and randomly struck rich and poor and young and old alike. "Danses macabres," allegories of equality before death, were at their height, in literature as well as in painting: in a scary and grotesque saraband, skeletons and corpses carry a hierarchy of living people—from the pope or monarch to a poor child, a bourgeois, or a scholar—along to their death. The theme dated back to before the plague, having emerged at the turn of the thirteenth and fourteenth centuries, but the pandemic caused it to appear in numerous churches in France, Germany, Switzerland, and England, and later in Italy. Several literary versions were composed throughout Europe, including the beautiful Spanish poem from the early fifteenth century, the *Danza general de la Muerte*.

These allegories of the dance of death that arose as a result of a deadly and uncontrollable epidemic are seen today as the final élan of an era, the Middle Ages, marked by man's awe before the unfathomable mysteries of the world and of life. It was a fear that could only be assuaged in the contemplation of beauty. This theme of the lugubrious saraband would endure until the early sixteenth century and the advent of the Renaissance. ⌛

FACING PAGE
GIOVANNI DONDI (1318–1389), *Mechanism and Gears of a Clock*, details of the Astrarium illustrated in the manuscript *Tractatus astrarii*, 1300s. Giovanni Dondi was a physician, poet, astronomer, and philosopher. Biblioteca Capitolare, Padua.

ABOVE
Filippo Brunelleschi (1377–1446), **CLOCK WITH WEIGHTS.** Museo Ideale Leonardo Da Vinci, Vinci.

WATCHMAKING
FROM 1300 TO 1500

In 1271, Robertus Anglicus, an English astronomer, wrote, "Clockmakers are trying to make a wheel which will make one complete revolution for every one of the equinoctial circle." In other words, these craftsmen were endeavoring to build a mechanism capable of automatically indicating the twenty-four "temporal" hours of the day, which had been established since antiquity and divided into twelve hours of daylight and twelve hours of darkness. By their very nature, these hours varied in length depending on the season.

Historians agree that the mechanical clock, featuring a combination of driving weight and cogwheels, both known since antiquity, and ancestors of the escapement, appeared between 1275 and 1285 in Flanders, Burgundy, England, and in the areas making up present-day Germany and Italy. Research to date has not provided more precise information about the name and birthplace of its inventor or inventors. The first mechanical clocks, whose lifespan did not exceed thirty years or so, have all been lost. Absent from scientific texts of the 1270s, their existence is attested in books written mostly in Latin, referred to by the term *horologium* or one of the numerous derivatives such as *oriole* and *orriulo*. All of these terms designate both a sundial and a water clock, and time-measuring devices in general, so there is much uncertainty about the characteristics of the objects mentioned. The picture only became clearer in the last quarter of the thirteenth century, with the English religious chronicles such as those of Dunstable Priory, Exeter Cathedral, and Canterbury Cathedral, and the account books of the king of France. Clocks also make their appearance in literature, implicitly in Jean de Meun's *Roman de la Rose* and explicitly in Dante's *Divine Comedy*, and in *L'Horloge amoureux*, a poem by Jean Froissart. However, no description of the earliest escapements has yet been found. This regulating mechanism—an essential part of mechanical devices and always used in traditional clock- and watchmaking—has the dual effect of suspending the action of the weight and the wheels at regular intervals and transferring energy to the balance to drive an alternating movement that divides time into equal parts.

The earliest cast-iron mechanisms installed in buildings were large and without a dial, and told the time by setting off a specific ringing of bells. A less costly type of clock involved a watchman sounding the hour on the main bell of a tower. These were set using a sundial, which was commonly used for this purpose until it was replaced by the telegraph and radio in the late nineteenth century.

The master clockmakers of the time enjoyed a truly encyclopedic knowledge: their special interest was astronomy and its instruments.

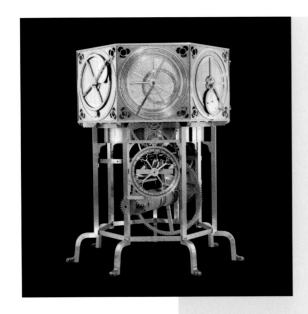

They saw the clock as the ideal means to ensure that the astrolabe would follow the movement of celestial bodies. At the time, religious life and civil life were closely connected. Astronomical timekeepers were installed in abbeys, cathedrals, and civil belfries. As symbols of modernity and economic power, these timepieces would spread swiftly through Europe during the fourteenth and fifteenth centuries: Norwich and Saint Albans in England; Strasbourg, Chartres, and Bourges in France; Frankfurt, Stralsund, Wismar, Villingen, Lübeck in Germanic lands; Lund in Sweden; Bern in Switzerland.

In Strasbourg Cathedral, the Three Kings clock, named for its three automaton Magi who parade by the Holy Family at noon, had a profound impact at the time. It served as a model for numerous monumental clocks up until the twentieth century. Lavishly decorated, with delicately painted statuettes, its mechanism worked an astrolabe, a calendar marked the 366 days of a leap year, and it had a chime. It is largely famous today for its rooster, considered the oldest preserved automaton. An exceptional specimen of medieval ironwork, the rooster beats its wings, raises its head, lowers its tail, and crows.

The political powers soon sought to equip themselves with timekeepers of their own. In Italy, Ubertino da Carrara had an impressive astronomical clock, constructed by Jacopo Dondi, installed on the façade of his Palazzo del Capitano. Gian Galeazzo Visconti, Duke of Milan, installed the astrarium (or planetarium) by Giovanni Dondi, Jacopo's son, at his castle in Pavia. This mechanical astrolabe, lost today, showed the hour, as well as the movements, according to Ptolemy's geocentric model, of the seven planets known at the time. The work was extremely famous and all the great princes, including Charles V, came to admire it. Charles V of France had public clocks installed at his residences in France, including his palace in Paris, opposite the Louvre. All of them sounded the hours, structuring the life of Parisians. In Prague, the city hall was equipped with an astronomical clock, complete—unusually for a civil building—with a liturgical calendar and a scene with automata representing the apostles of Christ.

Very few indoor clocks were built, however. Only kings, powerful lords, wealthy religious communities, and certain merchants had the financial means to own one. Indoor clocks made their appearance simultaneously in southern Germany, England, and Italy. In the 1430s, the pillars of a clock's cage were adorned with decorative bases and cast-iron pinnacles typical of Gothic architecture. The hours were painted in Gothic Roman numerals on a dial that was often ring-shaped and sometimes showed the lunar phases. Surmounting the clock was a bell in a bell tower

QVI DEDIT ANTE DVAS
TRIPLICEM DABIT ILLE
CORONAM

MACHINA QVÆ BIS SEX
TAM JVSTE DIVIDIT HORAS
JVSTITIAM SERVARE MONET
LEGES QVE TVERI

decorated with painted-metal floral motifs. These clocks served as a sign of wealth and as such would often be depicted in portraits of the owner.

In the early fifteenth century, the earliest uses of a coiled spring to drive the clock mechanism are attributed to the goldsmith Filippo Brunelleschi, who would later earn fame as the architect of the huge cupola of Florence's Santa Maria del Fiore Cathedral. The use of an internal driving weight led to the indoor clock, and that of the coiled spring to the portable clock and to the watch. These parallel developments characterized the timepieces of the Renaissance. **DOMINIQUE FLÉCHON**

THE TIME OF THE
RENAISSANCE

When, in the fall of 1494, the twenty-three-year-old painter Albrecht Dürer decided to take leave of his wife and Nuremberg for a while to see the painters of Venice, his city was one of the most culturally resplendent of Europe. A year earlier, the cosmographer and navigator Martin Behaim had presented his *Erdapfel*, the oldest known terrestrial globe and doubtless one of the last not to show North America, to the municipal council of Nuremberg. The city, a flourishing commercial center of Bavaria known for its goldsmiths and armorers, was also famous for a new specialty: the illustrated book. The recent inventions of Gutenberg in Mainz—cast-metal type and the printing press—in around 1450, rapidly spread throughout Europe: twenty million books were printed on the continent during the following half-century. In Nuremberg, printers managed to overcome the difficulties of producing books with both text from type and images from woodcuts. The young Dürer, already an extremely gifted painter and draftsman by the age of thirteen, had studied under the painter Michael Wolgemut, who taught him the secrets of the great Flemish painters as well as the art of woodcut. He would become a painter and printmaker.

It is not known if Dürer discovered Venetian painting in his own city or during the tour of Alsace and Switzerland that would qualify him as a master of his craft. Whatever the case, the art of Venice made a deep impression on him. He might have followed the obvious path of the great Flemish masters, but instead he was the first German painter to assimilate the principles of the movement, originating in Florence, known as the *Rinascità*. More than a renaissance, this term was in use from the fifteenth century to describe a full-blown humanist cultural revolution, which impacted the arts, literature, science, and everyday life.

In Venice, where he stayed until 1495, Dürer spent time at the studios of Carpaccio, Mantegna, and, above all, Bellini, taking in their new artistic ideas and participating in their research. In a scientific and classically inspired spirit that broke with medieval pictorial tradition, these artists were interested primarily with the depiction of the nude, the use of perspective, the effects of light and distance, and the realistic depiction of landscape. In the following years, with the increasing use of the canvas, the work of Leonardo da Vinci would solve almost all these difficulties of pictorial depiction.

During Dürer's stay at the Fondaco dei Tedeschi, Venice had for two centuries been the foremost Mediterranean trading city, thanks to its merchant galleys. Its warehouses were filled with goods purchased in the East—spices, cotton, silk, and sugar as well as cereals, wine, and wood—which it sold on throughout northern Europe. With its polychrome *palazzi* in Venetian-Byzantine and then Flamboyant Gothic styles built by the great patrician families along the Grand Canal, Saint Mark's Basilica, and the Doge's Palace, Venice was also the most majestic city of Europe. Dürer could marvel at the first Renaissance edifice of the city: the Dario palace by the architect Pietro Lombardo, completed circa 1490. Another Renaissance-style palace, Ca' Vendramin Calergi, was under construction, designed by Mauro Codussi, who, two years after Dürer's sojourn, would go on to build the Corner

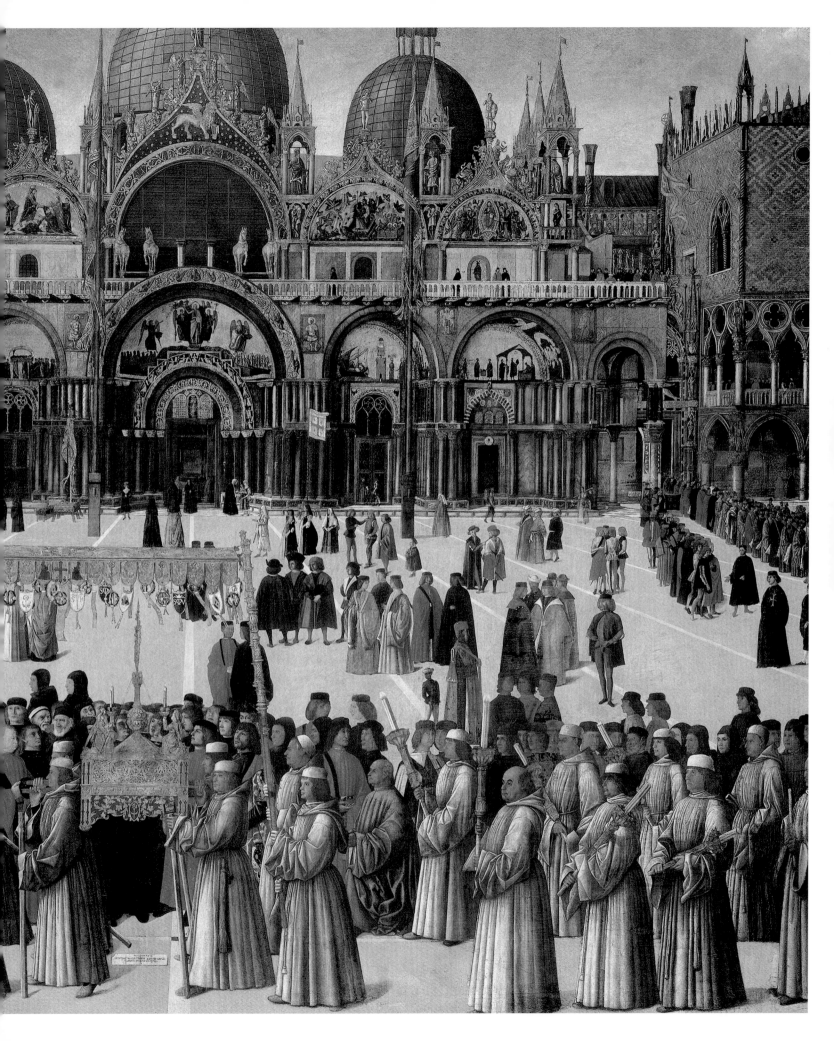

PAGES 44–45
Two works by **JEAN TOUTIN**
(1578–1644), a French master enamelist,
jeweler, and engraver. Page 44:
miniature for an oval gold watch case,
enameled in black and white, c. 1620.
Page 45: an engraving showing
a scene animated with figures, 1619.
Victoria and Albert Museum, London.

———

ABOVE
RAPHAEL (1483–1520), *Portrait
of Pope Leo X with Cardinals Luigi
de' Rossi and Giulio de' Medici*, 1518.
Galleria degli Uffizi, Florence.

———

FACING PAGE
MINIATURE TURRET CLOCK, 1538,
France. The finely worked, gilded
hexagonal case depicts allegories
of the heavenly bodies on five sides:
the Sun, Moon, Jupiter, Mars, and
Venus. The sixth side features
the single-hand dial. Beyer Zurich
Clock and Watch Museum.

Spinelli palace. With its classical inspiration, pillars, symmetrical design, and floor-length French windows, these were the years when the Renaissance began to take shape in Venice, inspired by Vitruvius's treatise *De architectura*.

A painting by Gentile Bellini, *Procession in Saint Mark's Square*, 1496–1500, shows us the square as Dürer would have seen it: the Procuratie Nuove, on the south side, had not yet been built, and the Procuratie Vecchie, on the north side, were still those erected in the twelfth century in the Venetian-Byzantine style, and would be destroyed by a fire twenty years later. The magnificent clock tower does not appear in the painting; Dürer could only have seen it on his second visit, in 1505. Its construction, in the Renaissance style of its architect, probably Mauro Codussi once more, began in 1496 and lasted three years. In this city of merchants and seafarers, twenty years before the appearance of the first wearable timepieces, it became essential to have a monumental public clock, replacing that of Saint Mark's Basilica, which was in a very poor state and considered irreparable. The new clock tower commissioned by the Republic of Venice was designed to display its power and splendor and was inaugurated on February 1, 1499. The great ultramarine dial of the astronomical clock was set over the arch of the passage between Saint Mark's Square and the Mercerie shopping streets leading to the Rialto. Above it is a statue of the Virgin Mary and the Infant Jesus, surmounted by the winged lion of Saint Mark, and, at the top of the tower, a pair of bronze figures, the "Moors," (originally gilded), which strike the hours on a bronze bell. The entire timekeeping mechanism, including these

automata and others—the Magi and an angel with a trumpet, which appear at Epiphany and on Ascension Day, moving in procession past the Virgin—and the astronomical clock itself, were the work of two clockmaker brothers, Gian Paolo and Gian Carlo Rainieri. The dial of the astronomical clock showed the twenty-four hours of the day in Roman numerals, the relative positions of Saturn, Jupiter, Mars, Venus, and Mercury, the phases of the moon, and the position of the sun in the zodiac. A weight system and foliot escapement controlled all of the automata. This masterpiece would be restored several times during the following centuries.

That same year, 1499, in Rome, Michelangelo gave the world his *Pietà*, with his lamenting Virgin far more beautiful than sorrowful. About ten years later, he started to decorate the ceiling of the Sistine Chapel, by request of Pope Julius II, with a dazzling Genesis steeped in the humanist ideal.

The sixteenth century saw the flourishing of a new aesthetic, as well as the enlightened "discovery" of the "New World" and a heightened interest in the ancient worlds. Both were a source of avid interest in Europe. The search for lucrative, rare, and precious products, profitable investments in weapons and shipbuilding, the desire to evangelize the world, progress in art and navigation, and new lands to be distributed to landless aristocrats all explain the Europeans' passion for long-distance voyages during this period. After Christopher Columbus opened the route to the Americas, and Vasco de Gama, that of the Indies, Magellan and then his navigator Elcano completed the first circumnavigation of the globe between 1519 and 1522.

These discoveries, followed by colonization, proved disastrous for the conquered populations, often nearly destroyed by imported diseases, the slave trade, and the annihilation of their religions and cultures. In Europe, the consequences were quite the opposite: Europeans' horizons were broadened, while knowledge of geography, cosmography, and cartography, climatology, and ethnology progressed considerably. From 1530, Copernicus's heliocentric theory began to gain recognition, although it would take several decades to take hold. An increase in wealth brought new refinements to the lifestyle of aristocrats and the more affluent middle classes. Europeans were introduced to crops such as tomato and vanilla, potato and maize, and enthusiastically adopted tea, coffee, cacao, and tobacco, not to mention silk and porcelain. The influx of gold and silver from South American mines led to a boom in fine metalwork and clockmaking.

Powerful figures were often patrons and collectors. In Florence in the second half of the fourteenth century, Lorenzo de' Medici was a leading example, providing support for Verrocchio and his pupil Leonardo da Vinci, Botticelli, Ghirlandaio, and a fifteen-year-old Michelangelo, whom he raised like his own son. He also promoted the development of Neoplatonism in art, thanks to his library of rediscovered ancient texts. After Julius II, the popes were also great patrons of the arts: Leo X commissioned Raphael to paint his portrait and the reception rooms in the papal apartments in the Vatican, while Paul III named Michelangelo his official architect and commissioned several portraits from Titian.

The French king Francis I was one of the greatest patrons of his time, protector of the arts and letters as well as ideas: he founded the Collège de France with the great humanist Guillaume Budé, and sponsored poets such as Clément Marot. He brought the Italian Renaissance to France, with Andrea del Sarto, Benvenuto Cellini, and the elderly Leonardo da Vinci, who, it is said, died in his arms. By asking Rosso Fiorentino and later Primaticcio and Nicolò dell'Abbate to decorate the Château de Fontainebleau, he created the first School of Fontainebleau. Francis was a great collector and purchased works by Michelangelo, Titian, and Raphael, among others. His sister, Marguerite de Navarre, a woman of letters herself, took the great Rabelais under her protection. These patrons not only promoted a genuine taste for art among princes and high-ranking citizens but also ushered in a new cultural and sociological phenomenon: the newly prestigious status of the artist, now a respected figure. Whether it actually happened or not, the image of Charles V picking up the brush of his protégé Titian is, in this respect, revealing, as is the (established) fact of Titian's being knighted by the king.

In central Europe, Emperor Rudolf II of Hapsburg had a voracious appetite for works of art, scientific instruments, and any precious or exotic objects that might be part of a "cabinet of curiosities" or *Kunstkammer*. This phenomenon of the private collection, displayed in one or several rooms of the home of a prince, scholar, or enlightened amateur emerged in the Renaissance. Rudolf's *Kunstkammer* in his castle in Prague, where he lived

from 1583, comprised several rooms, including a number of secret ones containing all kinds of strange artifacts reflecting his taste for esotericism and alchemy. Over the years, this cabinet of curiosities came to house the richest artistic and scientific collection in Renaissance Europe: ancient Greco-Roman bronzes and marbles, medallions, seashells, animal skeletons, crosses, vases, cups, weapons, jewelry, clocks, terrestrial globes, and all sorts of scientific instruments, not to mention precious stones, and, in a great room, an extraordinary collection of paintings, which Rudolf liked to examine by torchlight, alone in the evening. Court painter Arcimboldo made several of his signature fruit-and-vegetable portraits of the emperor, and served as his artistic adviser, responsible for bringing back from Italy or elsewhere the works of Rudolf's favored painters: Cranach the Elder, Titian, Correggio, Leonardo, Parmigianino, and, above all, Brueghel the Elder and Dürer, whom he worshipped and all of whose work he would have liked to own. In the meantime, he kept dozens of other painters from Italy, Germany, and the Netherlands busy with commissions.

Everything was a source of enthusiasm and wonder for the grandson of Charles V, be it philosophy, botany, zoology, mechanics, or precious metalwork. However, he had inherited from his uncle Philip II of Spain, with whom he had spent all of his teenage years in Madrid, a special taste for time-measuring instruments and clock automata: the king of Spain owned, at the time of his death, a collection of 104 automata and clocks. An inventory drawn up shortly before Rudolf's death suggests that he had collected almost two hundred

clocks and scientific instruments. In 1577, he commissioned an artistic clock from one of the most brilliant clockmakers of the day, Hans Schlottheim, active in Augsburg in Bavaria. He must have been happy with it, because five years later, he met the master clockmaker during a visit to Augsburg and placed further orders to add to his *Kunstkammer*.

In 1586, Schlottheim delivered to Rudolf in Prague an astonishing, galleon-shaped automaton clock in finely chased gilt brass, probably part of the order placed four years earlier. The emperor almost certainly chose the shape, as the galleon was depicted in many of Brueghel the Elder's drawings. The modernity and function of the ship would have appealed to him, too: the galleon, a cross between a sailing ship and a galley, was a recent vessel used in the precious metals trade between the New World and Spain. But it was also a warship, and many galleons would take part in the Spanish Armada two years later. The presence, in the form of a wooden figurine of Charles V, shown on the deck seated on his throne, suggests Rudolf may have intended this masterpiece to celebrate the conquest of Tunis by his grandfather fifty years earlier.

It is an extraordinary piece of work. Set on small, almost invisible wheels, the galleon measures about 3 ft. (1 m) high with its masts, and 27 ½ in. (70 cm) from bow to stern. It is armed with two batteries of guns. Several painted wooden figurines stand on the deck. At the foot of the mainmast is a clock with a dial decorated with plant motifs surmounted by the imperial double-headed eagle and flanked by two pillars of Hercules, part of the

emperor's coat of arms. The figure of the emperor sits under a baldachin wearing a crown and holding the imperial scepter and orb. Before him stand three heralds, and behind the throne, ready to step forward thanks to a clever mechanism, are seven prince electors of the empire. Guards are posted on either side of the throne and on the forecastle. Three sailors look ready to hoist the staysail, and four lookouts are in the mast tops. In addition, a few courtiers appear, alongside a group of ten trumpeters, a drummer, and a timpanist. The dragon-headed bowsprit, the arcaded forecastle and quarterdeck, masts, shrouds, and sails complete this magical evocation of an imperial galleon.

The mechanism is triggered by a small lever. Immediately, one of the lookouts starts to strike the twelve hours on his maintop shaped like an inverted bell. The heralds and electors then emerge from a door and pass before the emperor, who turns his head and raises his scepter to salute each one, while imperial music—the piece that always accompanied the emperor's public appearances—is performed by the trumpets and two kettle drums. Then the sailors hoist the sails, the rudder starts to flap, and, to the sound of a drum, the ship starts to move. Finally, a dozen cannon fire. After a minute of this fascinating voyage, the music and the galleon come to a stop.

Known as the "Nef de Charles Quint," this automaton clock is kept today at the Musée National de la Renaissance at the Château d'Écouen. In its combination of artistic elegance and extreme ingenuity, its evocation of conquests and maritime trade, its mixture of music and firing guns, it perfectly encapsulates the Renaissance and its ambiguities. ⌛

PAGES 58–59
HIERONYMUS FRANCKEN II (1578–1623) and JAN BRUEGHEL THE ELDER (1568–1625), *Albert VII, Archduke of Austria, and the Archduchess Isabella Clara Eugenia Visiting the Collection of Pierre Roose*, c.1621–23. Walters Art Museum, Baltimore.

———

FACING PAGE
Mechanical galleon called THE NEF DE CHARLES QUINT, c. 1586, gilt brass clock and automata, enamel, and iron, attributed to Hans Schlottheim (c. 1545–1626). Made to entertain guests between courses at a banquet, this three-masted galleon comes to life at the chiming of a bell and plays a miniature organ hidden within the hull. Musée national de la Renaissance, Écouen.

———

ABOVE
MIGUEL OCAÑA (1840–1919), *King Charles V at Yuste*. In this nineteenth-century painting, Charles V (1500–1558), is surrounded by monks and observes the automata made by Juanelo Turriano (1501–1585), an engineer and inventor, who is also portrayed alongside him. Museo Nacional del Prado, Madrid.

WATCHMAKING
FROM 1500 TO 1675

The spring mechanism, as adapted to clockmaking in the early fifteenth century, was slow to develop. The reason for this was no doubt the double difficulty of enabling it to retain sufficient force to resist the friction of the first cogs and balance its tension in relation to the degree to which it was wound.

The small table clocks produced in the early Renaissance were, in both design and decoration, of very high quality. Miniature versions could be worn around the neck, suspended from a chain or inside a garment. The first portable clock or watch appeared circa 1475. With or without a chime, it was mentioned in Italy in a letter dated July 19, 1488, written by Jacopo Trotti, ambassador at the court of Milan. Shortly afterward, reference was made to it in parts of France, the Germanic lands, and in Geneva. The first watches took either the spherical form of the pomander, an openwork pendant containing musk, or that of a small drum. Soon they became oval, octagonal, square, or were made in the shape of a star, a Latin cross, or a skull. Some were inspired by the animal kingdom—dog, shell, dolphin, rabbit, lion, bird—and others by the plant world—tulip buds and other flowers.

Ornamental flat or relief engraving of watch and table-clock cases, dials, and mechanisms attained a degree of absolute mastery. Various enameling techniques were progressively applied, alone or in combination, while painting on enamel appeared in the early 1630s. German, French, Dutch, and Swiss engravers and enamelers all used the motifs found in books of prints by the likes of Virgil Solis, Étienne Delaune, and Theodor de Bry. These common sources explain the stylistic unity of timepieces at the time.

The spring-driven Renaissance clock, known as the table clock, borrowed much from architecture. It often took the form of a cylindrical, square, or pentagonal tower, topped with an elegant openwork dome to ensure the even diffusion of the sound of its chime. Some were made in the shape of a fort or baptistery. Certain mechanisms were fitted into books, monstrances, or in the base of a crucifix. The most sophisticated designs came from southern Germany, most notably Augsburg, Nuremberg, and Ulm. Of extremely high artistic and technical quality, certain clocks provided complex astronomical indications, while others featured automata. They served as diplomatic gifts and were always the

pride of the popes and European, Chinese, and Ottoman rulers who gave and received them. When set on formal Western dining tables, they provided entertainment between courses for guests at court. Some were relatively simple in design, such as a dancing-bear master who moves his head while restraining the bear, who in turn looks about to leap, its aggressiveness conveyed in powerful movements of the head and eyes. Others were incredibly complex: Diana the Huntress rides a deer whose body is a receptacle filled with wine. A feasting Bacchus lounges on a chariot drawn by elephants to the sound of music. Nefs with sailors in the rigging carry a host of figures gathered around an unnamed dignitary; they move forward in a rolling, pitching motion, until the ship's cannon fires, inviting the nearest guest to empty his cup.

During the Renaissance, astrological factors were taken into account before any important decision. Surgeons, for example, would use the "time of the stars" to help them in their choice of incision, as well as the time and date of the surgery. For surgery to take place, neither the moon nor the planet associated with the organ to be operated on could be in an unfavorable position. Because of this, indoor astrolabe clocks of the sixteenth and seventeenth centuries appear to have been designed primarily to write horoscopes. Their relatively simple mechanisms were sufficiently accurate to show, in real time, the position of the fixed stars in relation to the planets. At the same time, the study of the movements of celestial bodies played a crucial role in moving from Ptolemy's geocentric model to the Copernican system, and enabled Johannes Kepler to establish his famous three laws. Precious celestial globes and spheres built between 1550 and 1650 by the great Renaissance masters proved extremely useful in this research. Joost Bürgi, pioneer of algebra and logarithms, astronomer and clockmaker, was the first to use the second as a unit for measuring time. Under the influence of Kepler, he built in 1623 the first known modern planetary clock whose clockmaking technology and decoration formed a harmonious ensemble. The case and cupola, both in rock crystal, were mounted on an openwork gilt bronze base containing a mechanism that was among the very first to display the hours, minutes, and seconds. In addition, it operated a sphere containing a clockwork movement that animated a small sun according to the star's movement. This rock-crystal sphere engraved with the constellations is attributed to the Milanese Ottavio Miseroni, considered the most talented lapidary of his time.

In the wealthy cities of the Renaissance, an elegant, light style of architecture gradually began to replace the earlier Gothic style. The most famous edifices, whether religious, such as in Strasbourg, Augsburg, and

FACING PAGE
Hans Buschmann, **HERCULES AND THE CELESTIAL VAULT,** Renaissance table clock, c. 1630, Augsburg. The silver statuette of Hercules bears the celestial vault on which feature the various indications of time, including average solar time, and the age and phases of the moon. On the base, silver rings indicate the day of the week, date, and month. Beyer Zurich Clock and Watch Museum.

———

BELOW
Jacques de La Garde (fl. 1551–1565), **SPHERICAL NECKLACE WATCH,** 1551. Gilt brass and iron, featuring a case made of two engraved hemispheres which open by a hinge, this watch is considered to be the oldest dated and signed watch. Musée du Louvre, Paris.

Lyon, or civic, like those in Venice, Olomouc, and Ulm, featured monumental clocks with an astrolabe or a zodiac dial. All of them served to symbolize power—as did, in a different manner, the clock installed on both sides of an arcade over one of the main streets in Rouen at the time, with its flamboyant dials, moon globes, and allegorical figures for the days of the week. But although the Renaissance produced some outstanding technical and decorative masterpieces, precision in clockwork mechanisms was yet to be invented. **D.F.**

THE TIME OF THE
GRAND SIÈCLE

By 1690, Paris had supplanted Rome as the artistic and cultural capital of Europe. That year, Jules Hardouin-Mansart, "first architect" to Louis XIV, completed the construction of the façades around Place Vendôme in Paris, a majestically classical architectural tribute to the glory of his king. The marquis de Louvois, who had designed the square six years earlier as a pendant to the Place des Victoires that was under construction at the time, supervised the building work, which required the demolition of the Hôtel de Vendôme and the Capuchin convent to be moved. As the successor to Colbert, Superintendent of Buildings, Arts and Manufactories, Louvois was also in charge of the construction of the Château de Versailles. And in his capacity of Secretary of State for War, which he had been since 1677, he was the most powerful minister of the kingdom.

In 1690, Louvois took delivery of a masterpiece that he had commissioned several months earlier from André-Charles Boulle, the king's cabinetmaker, who for ten years had been making a small fortune executing numerous orders for Versailles: a clock with pedestal, decorated with the marquetry for which he was famous, in oak, tin, brass, and tortoiseshell. The clock—of a kind known as a "religieuse" at the time, for its plain, cubic shape—with its tapered pedestal reminiscent of a table leg, stood 7 ft. (2.2 m) tall. The ensemble was lavishly decorated with delicately chased gilt bronze motifs, with four sphinxes supporting the clock, a female mask—perhaps Minerva, goddess of war—in the center of the pendulum door, acanthus leaves, flaming urns, and so on. Boulle drew

inspiration for this decor, as he often did, from the drawings of Jean Berain, designer to the king and author of thousands of decorative motifs for cabinetmaking, goldsmithery, tapestry making, and interior design, and even the figureheads and sterns of the royal navy ships.

For the clock itself, and part of its decoration, Boulle turned to one of the best clockmakers in Paris, Isaac Thuret, "clockmaker in ordinary to the king." Thuret also happened to be his neighbor: like Boulle, he had lodgings and a studio at the Louvre, a privilege granted by the king to his best craftsmen. Thuret had long been responsible for the adjusting of the instruments at the Académie des Sciences, where he worked with one of its eminent members, the Dutch scientist and mathematician Christiaan Huygens. Inventor in 1657 of the pendulum clock, Huygens asked Thuret in 1675 to build the first watch with a coiled balance spring, another of his inventions. For Louvois' pendulum clock, Thuret designed an eight-day, spring-wound movement, chiming every quarter hour and equipped with a barometer whose indications were arranged in a semi-circle over the female mask: TOURMENT, PLUVIEUX, CHANGEANT, BEAU TEMPS, TRÈS SEC (Stormy, Rainy, Changeable, Fine, Very Dry). The dial is in chased gilt brass, edged with Arabic numerals in enamel.

With its impressive size, sumptuous harmony, balance and symmetry, and Greco-Roman references, this clock is a magnificent illustration of seventeenth-century classicism and in particular the Louis XIV style, which had to reflect royal power, munificence, and majesty. Louvois may have

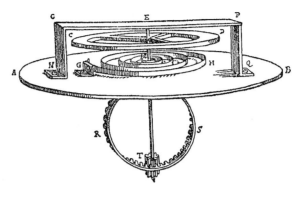

commissioned it for his recently acquired Château de Montfort in Burgundy. But was it really suited to this austere medieval fortress? It was much more at home in his apartments in the Hôtel de la Surintendance, which at the time was separated by a gallery from the Château de Versailles, and where he was most often in residence. Whatever the case, he was unfortunately not able to contemplate it for long: he died suddenly the following year at the age of fifty, apparently of a stroke. Boulle and Thuret would build a small series of clocks after this model, including one kept today at the Metropolitan Museum of Art in New York.

In 1690, France was at war. It had been for decades, even centuries, but never had it known so many conflicts as under Louis XIV, imbued as he was with his own glory and certain that his military victories could only enhance it further. That year, France was fighting almost all of Europe, which had formed an opposing coalition—the League of Augsburg—in a war that would last for seven years, with terrible consequences for the country: the considerable deterioration of public finances, more or less compensated for by new taxes, as well as an agricultural crisis, food shortages, and an epidemic that would cause two million deaths. And yet, France remained the leading military, political, and demographic power in Europe. For thirty years, thanks to its royal navy and its great shipping companies, it had managed to impose a strong political and commercial presence in North America and Asia, creating the first French colonial empire: New France in Canada, Louisiana, and the Antilles, and trading posts in India and Réunion brought

France new resources thanks to the sugar and spice trade. For thirty years the nation's royal power and its shrewd ministers Colbert, then Louvois, had ensured the spread of its influence in every sphere, particularly artistic and cultural. The king loved the arts, especially when they reflected his grandeur. In the first twenty years of his reign, through the intervention of Colbert, he acquired four hundred works of art, paintings, and sculptures. His collection of classical antiquities at Versailles, made up of originals and copies, was displayed in the Marble Courtyard, the Royal Courtyard, the Grande Galerie, in various reception rooms, and in the gardens. In the meantime, a cultural and artistic movement was emerging in France, initially inspired by the Italian artists, which would influence the whole of Louis XIV's "Grand Siècle" ("great century") and would spread throughout Europe: classicism.

After the short-lived glory of the Château de Vaux-le-Vicomte, the Château de Versailles, built from 1661 by the same architect, Louis Le Vau, on the site of a Louis XIII hunting lodge, became the principal embodiment of French "Grand Siècle" classicism. When the royal court moved in there in 1682, the palace was not yet completed, but already the Le Nôtre-designed gardens, the Grand Canal, the great apartments decorated by Le Brun, and the Ministers' Wings built by Hardouin-Mansart all illustrated this taste for formal harmony within a strict layout, governed by a sense of grandeur and omnipresent references to the ancient world, and enlivened with extraordinary baroque decors. Completed two years later, the

Hall of Mirrors, the work of Hardouin-Mansart and Le Brun, would complete the whole, in a majestic illumination that seemed more like an ode to the Sun—synonymous with splendor but also with truth—than to reason.

Rarely has a monarch been as successful as Louis XIV in associating the art of his time with his own person. Versailles was at the time the foremost setting of French classical art, whether visual, literary, or musical. The famous 1701 portrait of the king in his coronation robes by Hyacinthe Rigaud illustrates how consummately "official" painting had become. Extremely staged in its composition and setting, representing the majesty of the king in every detail, playing cleverly with the light to bring out the solar symbolism, this painting—which Louis XIV hung at Versailles as soon as it was completed—remains one of the major examples of French pictorial classicism. It was a classicism that had been formalized some time earlier by Charles Le Brun, "first painter to the king," appointed by Colbert in 1663 as director of the Académie Royale de Peinture et de Sculpture. In a series of lectures, this authoritative "chief painter" set out his theory of classicism, almost entirely inspired by the work of Nicolas Poussin. Born in 1594 and died in 1665 in Rome, Poussin would exercise a considerable influence on the next generation of French classical painters, who no doubt drew inspiration from his ideas on art and painting: "My natural tendency forces me to look for and like well-ordered things, fleeing confusion which I find to be contrary and the enemy, as is the light to dark shadows."[1] And,

"The painter must begin with disposition, then ornament, decorum, beauty, grace, vivacity, costume, vraisemblance, and judgment in every part."[2]

In one of his lectures, Charles Le Brun also stressed the importance of Poussin's classical inspiration. Philippe de Champaigne, who was superseded by Le Brun, his junior by a few years, was another example of the official painter, executing no fewer than eleven portraits of Richelieu. Of a more religious inspiration, his painting nevertheless remains one of the most powerful and fascinating of this century in France, notably in the expressive depth of his portraits.

In French neoclassical theatre, which followed the three unities derived from Aristotle and laid down by Nicolas Boileau—*may a single complete action, in one place and one day, occupy the stage until the end*—Jean Racine, classical tragedian par excellence, had close connections with the court and had been in the king's regular employment since 1663. *Iphigénie* was first performed in Versailles in 1674. Twenty years later, Racine was appointed "historian to the king" and Louis XIV granted him lodgings at the chateau. Molière used everyday, even familiar language, and yet he, too was steeped in classicism: he was inspired by writers from the ancient world, such as Terence and Plautus, and sometimes wrote in alexandrines, seeking always to formalize the freedom of farce, until the ultimate honor of being received at Versailles, where he performed practically all of his plays before the king. Often he would be accompanied by the music of Jean-Baptiste Lully, superintendent of royal music, who provided music for the king to

dance to. A notable exception to these courtly customs, Jean de La Fontaine, despite being one of the greatest French poets of all times, would pay all his life for having been in the service of and for having defended Nicolas Fouquet, the man removed from Vaux-le-Vicomte and imprisoned for life by the king. Protected by the duchesse d'Orléans, and later Marguerite de La Sablière, and inspired by ancients such as Aesop, Horace, and Livy, he wrote his *Fables*, which were classic in their form and moral, and whose combination of natural ease, rhythm, and purity of style was truly brilliant.

The splendor of the reign of Louis XIV also manifested itself in the elegance of the products made by the Royal Manufactories, which the king asked Jean-Baptiste Colbert to create or develop. There were about fifteen of them in existence, between 1663 and the death of the sovereign in 1715. The idea was not only to promote the economic and commercial development of the country, but also to develop its artistic and cultural reputation throughout Europe, thanks to precious and well-made products that would demonstrate, for many years to come, in the lavish interiors of the international elite, what Voltaire would call French *grand goût* (elegant taste). Among these fine artifacts were carpets from the Savonnerie, tapestries from the Gobelins, Beauvais, and Arbusson manufactories, mirrors, crystal, and glasswork from Saint-Gobain, Portieux, and Vallérysthal, fine linens from Abbeville, Villeneuvette, and Les Saptes, and lace from Auxerre. The proactive Colbert had no hesitation in recruiting, sometimes at extremely high cost, craftsmen and manufacturers from neighboring countries, if they were reputed to be the best: the Dutch

LEFT
SIMON RENARD DE SAINT-ANDRÉ
(1613–1677), *Louis XIV Visits the Gobelins Manufacture on October 15, 1667*, late 1600s. The celebrated French portraitist is remembered above all for his Vanitas paintings. Châteaux de Versailles et de Trianon, Versailles.

RIGHT
RIGHT
CHRISTIAN BERENTZ (1658–1722),
Still Life with a Pocket Watch,
1700–1722. Berenz was a baroque
painter born in Germany who lived in
Italy until his death. Galleria
Nazionale d'Arte Antica di Palazzo
Corsini, Rome.

cloth manufacturer Josse Van Robais was granted a loan of 80,000 livres and a gift of 20,000 livres, enabling him to establish the Abbeville manufactory, while Venetian craftsmen were hired to make mirrors for Saint-Gobain.

Colbert's catches not only served the interests of French industry and trade. For the greater glory of his king and the power of his country, in 1666 Colbert created the Académie Royale des Sciences, and endeavored to draw foreign scientists to France. The greatest of them at the time was Christiaan Huygens, who had inspired the mechanism in the clock made by Boulle and Thuret. When Colbert received him in Paris that same year, as a member of the new Académie, he had already invented the pendulum clock, the first accurate mechanical time-keeping device in history. Huygens received the highest allowance in the Académie, was the only academician to have lodgings in the King's Library, and remained in Paris for fifteen years. During this period he developed a clock-regulating system, this time for portable clocks or watches: the balance spring regulator. In January 1675, he had the first pocket watch equipped with this system made by

Isaac Thuret. By reducing a watch's daily variance to five minutes, at a time when it could often exceed half an hour, this invention brought about a revolution in the concept of time. "The gain in accuracy," wrote David S. Landes,[3] "brought watch performance very close to the standard we now employ in ordering life and work. The balance spring thus laid the material basis for what even we would consider punctuality."

Huygens fell ill in 1681 and decided to return to his family in The Hague, with plans to come back to Paris once he had recovered. The death of his protector, Colbert, in 1683, and the revocation of the Edict of Nantes two years later changed his mind. He continued with his research in The Hague until his death in 1695.

Louis XIV would go on to reign for another twenty years, and with his death the Grand Siècle came to an end. One of his greatest, yet rarely mentioned, achievements is to have radically transformed our relationship with time. Watches and clocks had become reliable, and therefore not only credible but also increasingly necessary. A new era was born. ⌛

FACING PAGE
Jacques Cogniet (1661–1731),
Louis XIV DECORATIVE CLOCK
with Boulle marquetry, late 1600s.
The dial is of chased bronze, with
twelve small enamel panels indicating
the hours. The mechanism drives
the hands and a striking-work
chimes the hours. Château de
Vaux-le-Vicomte, Maincy.

WATCHMAKING
FROM 1675 TO 1715

In seeking a way to replace the foliot regulator, which was at the origin of the mechanical clock but lacked precision, Galileo had the idea of applying the pendulum to the measurement of time. He explored its physical laws and designed a mechanism to regulate its movement. Being too elderly to build a prototype, he entrusted the task to his son Vincenzio, who died before he could finish it. The first pendulum clock was made by Salomon Coster, clockmaker in The Hague, following the instructions of Christiaan Huygens. Astronomer, mathematician, and physicist of high repute, invited to Paris by Colbert to further his research, Huygens is considered the father of scientific clockmaking. In abandoning the traditional foliot in favor of a pendulum that was inexpensive and separate from the gears, he achieved a fundamental and economical breakthrough, improving the accuracy of the best timekeepers from fifteen minutes per day to ten or fifteen seconds. On June 16, 1657, the States General of the Netherlands granted a patent for this invention, which opened the way to minute hands and second hands. Huygens believed he was capable of solving the "longitude problem," and hoped to see longitude used at sea, if only a clock could be designed for use on an unstable ship. His project would fail, however, as his later research showed. Yet the problem was a crucial one: the safety of sailors and merchant ships depended on it, ever since the first great maritime crossings in the late fifteenth century. The position or point of a ship, and, later, of an airplane, was defined by its geographical coordinates: latitude and longitude. The first corresponded to the height of the sun above the horizon at noon, which, since antiquity, had been calculated quite easily. To determine longitude, however, the Greek astronomer Hipparchus had already stated in the first century BCE that one would have to measure the difference between the time at the place of observation and the time at a prime meridian. In the absence of sufficiently precise instruments, seafarers had to use long and complicated methods of calculation based on astronomical observations, with their inherent risks of error, until the late eighteenth century. Huygens' invention of a coiled spring to regulate the movements of a watch's balance wheel came out of his quest for longitude. It was officially announced at the Société Royale de France in Paris on January 30,

1675, and its impact was similar to that of the use of the pendulum in the clock, which improved the daily variance of the most sophisticated watches from thirty or forty minutes per day to four or five minutes.

The pendulum regulator and the balance spring were major events in the history of clock- and watchmaking and would greatly boost the development of science and technology. The most sophisticated clocks that measured time to the second would show the influence of temperature and atmospheric pressure on accuracy. Research on these would lead to the thermometer and the barometer and to their international measuring scales.

Although still only rarely found in the homes of the wealthy, the pendulum clock gradually gained recognition, thanks to the keen interest of scientists. In order to accommodate its swinging pendulum, it was larger in size than the Renaissance table clock, and so it offered greater scope to decorators. The rather austere ebony or blackened pearwood cabinet housing the "religieuse" type of clock, which was adopted throughout Western Europe, was softened by brass filigree and engraved or chased motifs.

With the accession to the throne of the Sun King and the building of the Château de Versailles, the works of architects, interior designers, artists, and craftsmen would influence the tastes of high society. Cabinetmakers, bronze casters, engravers, and gilders all worked with clockmakers, who came up with a type of monumental pendulum clock with increasingly numerous and varied bronze ornaments in the baroque style. The ebony cabinet (or case) borrowed from the "religieuse" clock was brightened up with a rich and complex type of tortoiseshell marquetry inlaid with brass or tin, known as Boulle work even though André-Charles Boulle was not alone in producing it. Although Louis XIV clocks were designed to be placed on a piece of furniture or a mantelpiece, many of them stood on a corbel, a small matching console. The use of the pendulum also led to the appearance of the first floor or longcase clocks. Their tall case housed the long pendulum regulating the weight mechanism. Some of the more monumental ones featured spectacular gilt bronze decoration in both high and low relief as well as sculpture in the round.

During the course of the seventeenth century, developments in clockmaking techniques transformed the watch from an ornamental jewel into a timekeeper. Enamel painting, which emerged in the second quarter of the century, was immediately applied to watch decoration, because of its durability. Originally developed in Blois,

it spread throughout Europe thanks to the master enamelers, whose exceptional skills were put to use in work for the great monarchs. Among them were Jacques Bordier and Jean Petitot, Paul Prieur, and members of the Huaud and Thouron families. With the invention of the coiled spring, a type of watch characteristic of the Louis XIV period appeared in France. Called the *oignon* (onion) because of its shape and size, its case was either engraved and chased in the style of the ornamentalists of the time—Jean Berain, Pierre Bourdon, Jean Bourguet—or covered in shagreen or studded leather.

The year 1685 saw the revocation of the Edict of Nantes, which saw thousands of Protestant refugees forced to move to Germany, England, the Netherlands, and Switzerland, taking with them their culture, expertise, and French taste. **D.F.**

FACING PAGE
Jean-Pierre Huaud (1655–1723),
ROUND ENAMELED POCKET WATCH,
late 1600s. The enamel decorations
by the Huaud brothers are highly
decorative and of a remarkable
quality; they stand out for their
extraordinary detail and bright colors.
Musée du Louvre, Paris.

———

BELOW
FRENCH "ONION" WATCH with
alarm, late 1600s. Dial formed
of a ring enameled with black
Roman numerals. At the center,
the alarm dial of gilt and engraved
brass. The movement is signed
Nicolas Gribelin (1637–1719), Paris.
Musée international d'horlogerie,
La Chaux-de-Fonds.

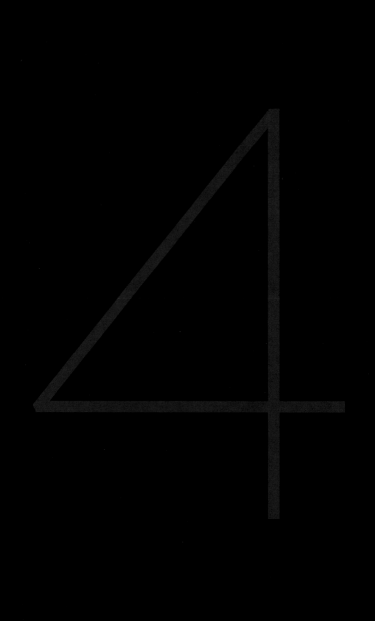

THE TIME OF THE
ENLIGHTENMENT

Between 1750 and 1752, two Parisian crafts-men, the goldsmith-enameler Charles-Simon Boucher and the clockmaker Jacques-Jérôme Gudin, produced a magnificent women's watch and chain. The guilloché and enameled gold watch case and chain were exquisitely graceful and refined, executed in the rocaille style that was in fashion at the time, suggesting a rose bush with pink flowers in bud or full bloom, and stems and leaves in a beautiful soft green. At the time, Gudin was just twenty years old. It would take him another ten years to qualify as a mas-ter of his craft and open his own studio on the banks of the Seine on the Quai des Orfèvres. He would become a clockmaker of repute, produc-ing watches, pendulum clocks, and wall clocks for high society, including the prince de Conti and the duc de Choiseul. But a single creation of his is kept in the Department of Decorative Arts at the Musée du Louvre: this rose watch and chain from his early years, whose original owner remains a mystery.

These pink roses inevitably call to mind the bright and beautiful marquise de Pompadour, born Jeanne-Antoinette Poisson, Louis XV's mistress since 1745. She adored flowers, to the extent that almost all known portraits of her, particularly the admirable works of François Boucher, depict her with roses. Pink was also her favorite color, and one she made fashionable at court. The Liège porcelain painter Philippe Xhrouet, who worked at the Sèvres royal porcelain factory, created a new color for her, Pompadour pink, a lilac pink that adorned numer-ous table services, as well as the biscuit-porcelain roses made by the manufactory—reputedly an idea of the marquise's, which she arranged in flowerbeds and sprayed with perfume.

Born in 1721, Madame de Pompadour is one of the most resplendent and most active figures of the spirit of the Enlightenment, which, in France, spanned the period from the death of Louis XIV to the Revolution. Many of the famed intellectuals and artists of the time benefited from her protection, particularly the most popu-lar among them, Voltaire. The man was known mostly in his lifetime for his tragedies, but the whole of France, even without reading his work, loved his scathing irony—that of his novels and stories, *Candide, Zadig, Micromégas*—aimed at the tyrannical, the intolerant, cruel potentates, or the clergy, among others. Eventually exiled, impris-oned, and banished from Versailles for his provoc-ative writings and speeches, Voltaire often worked from the neighboring countries of his native land. In 1734, he wrote his *Lettres philosophiques*, praising the freedom and tolerance that reigned in England, and today considered the true manifesto of the Enlightenment. Yet at the time, the text was burned in front of the Parlement de Paris and earned Voltaire a royal *lettre de cachet*, or arrest warrant, that forced him to flee France once more. However, Madame de Pompadour was an admirer, and obtained his par-don from Louis XV ten years later. Voltaire sub-sequently became a historiographer of the kingdom of France and was granted the title of "gentle-man in ordinary of the king's chamber." But the king did not like him, and Voltaire would soon

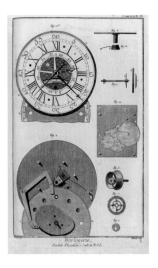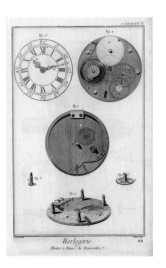

seek out a much more enlightened spirit, in the person of Frederick II, king of Prussia, a French speaker and Francophile.

Madame de Pompadour also sought the king's support for the monument of knowledge that was the *Encyclopédie*, edited by the writer and philosopher Denis Diderot and the mathematician and scientist Jean le Rond d'Alembert. The work, a scientific compilation of all branches of knowledge, which long encountered opposition from the Church and state authorities, advocated progress, freedom, and reason, and remains one of the major symbols of the French Enlightenment. Its seventeen volumes and ten volumes of illustrations were published between 1751 and 1772. Madame de Pompadour also ardently defended her friend Montesquieu, fiercely attacked after the publication in 1748 of one of his master-pieces, *De l'esprit des lois* (The Spirit of Laws). In it, the author of *Lettres persanes* (Persian Letters) drew an extremely detailed, and reasoned, picture of legal regimes and social organization throughout the world. Despite the controversies stirred up by con-servatives and ecclesiastics, in 1752 Madame de Pompadour posed for a magnificent pastel portrait by the painter Quentin de La Tour, standing by a table on which the third volume of her friend's con-troversial work can be seen. On the table are also the fourth volume of the *Encyclopédie* and an epic poem by Voltaire, *La Henriade*. All of the arts protected by the beautiful marquise are evoked in the painting, for Quentin de La Tour also shows a folder of draw-ings, and a musical score, which his model is leafing through. Naturally, she wears a sumptuous silk "robe à la française" woven with a pink rose motif.

The marquise was also a fervent admirer of Jean-Jacques Rousseau, the most fascinating figure of the Enlightenment in Europe. In 1753, in her Château de Bellevue in Meudon, southwest of Paris, she played the role of Colin in the one-act interlude *Le Devin du village* by Rousseau, whose work she had already seen performed with the king the previous year at Fontainebleau. At the time, Rousseau, who was born in 1712 in Geneva into a dynasty of clockmakers, had already written a num-ber of articles on music for the *Encyclopédie*, and three years earlier had published a paradoxical essay for which he became famous, *Discours sur les sciences et les arts*, in which—contrary to the spirit of the Enlightenment—he argued that the latter cor-rupted morality and prevented a clear awareness of the tyranny to which men are subject. In 1754 he published his *Discours sur l'origine et les fondements de l'inégalité parmi les hommes* (Discourse on the Origins and the Foundations of Inequality Among Men), in which he developed his idea of man born naturally good but corrupted by unjust society and private property. Two major works of Rousseau's were pub-lished eight years later: *Émile, ou De l'éducation*—a treatise on the nature of education that made a deep impression on Immanuel Kant—and *Du con-trat social*, a political-philosophical essay that, in defending the principles of popular sovereignty, equality, and liberty, would be one of the catalysts and major references of the French Revolution.

In eighteenth-century Europe, the French were not the only ones to be doing some thinking. Kant, an avid reader of Rousseau, developed his moral concept of "categorical imperative" with

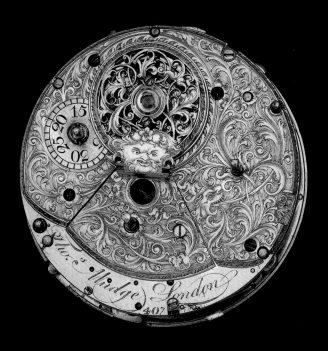

the publication in 1785 of the *Fundamental Principles of the Metaphysic of Morals*. A year earlier, Kant had been the first to theorize the very concept of "enlightenment," in the sense of an intellectual project, in his work *An Answer to the Question: What is Enlightenment?* For Kant, it was mostly about thinking for oneself, with courage and without prejudice, in reference to Horace's "*Sapere aude!*" (Dare to know). *Aufklärung* ("clarification" or "enlightenment") is an understanding or awareness, a liberation, and an emancipation. It is about thinking for oneself, becoming intellectually "of age," independent. "Enlightenment," Kant wrote, "is man's emergence from his self-incurred immaturity. Immaturity is the inability to use one's own understanding without the guidance of another."[1]

The Age of Enlightenment in Europe produced not only great philosophers but also authors of universal literary masterpieces. The Anglo-Irish writer Jonathan Swift, an Anglican cleric with a biting wit—who had already produced, with his *Tale of a Tub* in 1704, an extraordinary satire of all forms of human baseness, particularly fanaticism—won lasting fame for *Gulliver's Travels*, a philosophical and magical tale for children and adults alike, which achieves a highly subtle critique of British society. Among other writers of note are the Venetian Giacomo Casanova, who detested the French Revolution and yet remains an essential figure of this age, which is characterized, for some, by an insatiable taste for travel, freedom, and libertinism. The man with 122 female conquests—if not 142, according to some sources—not to mention a few male ones, wrote

his memoirs in French—*History of My Life*, an extraordinary succession of very real adventures experienced by a lover of amorous intrigue, gambling, music, beauty, and life in general. (It is worth noting that Count Jan Potocki, the Polish author of numerous ethnological works and an extraordinary novel, considered the only baroque novel of the Enlightenment period, *The Manuscript Found in Saragossa*, also wrote in French.)

It was also in France, where conversation had been elevated to an art form, that the phenomenon of the salon was most remarkable. Salons were usually hosted by a woman intellectual, who provided a venue for regular meetings of literati and artists of both sexes. Marie du Deffand, Marie-Thérèse Geoffrin, Julie de Lespinasse, and Germaine de Staël were among the most famous of salon hostesses. The salons sometimes led to boudoirs, where love affairs would be played out. In literature, architectural follies were often depicted as scenes of amorous pursuits as seen in works by the marquis de Sade, Crébillon fils, or Choderlos de Laclos. Amorous play, wit, intrigue, a taste for intellectual jousting as well as for the arts and fine objects—such frivolous pleasures, all in a certain spirit of obliviousness to political and social threats, characterized the state of mind of the aristocratic and, to a lesser degree, middle-class elites. It was a state of mind that favored the arts and required a comfortable, elegant setting filled with art works, objects and ornaments, game tables, and musical instruments. It was a state of mind expressed through a sensual, feminine idea of beauty.

A famous painting encapsulates the frenetic libertinage of high society in this period: *The Bolt*, by the painter Jean-Honoré Fragonard, a pupil of François Boucher, who had the bright idea—because it quickly became a lucrative business—of specializing in bawdy or licentious scenes. In this painting, which today hangs in the Louvre, a man in shirt sleeves, with his shoes already removed, closes the bolt of the door with his right hand while grasping in his left, not without a degree of brutality, a woman pretending to resist. The two figures are disheveled, their clothes half undone. In the man's ardor and the woman's predictable abandon, and the as-yet untouched apple shown to the left of the canvas, there is a certain eroticism. But Fragonard was a great painter, and his painting's composition, with its combined visual and psychological energy, juxtaposition of the still and the animated, and play of light and shadow, make *The Bolt* a masterpiece. The art historian Daniel Arasse identified a number of signs incorporated by Fragonard on the left side of the picture—"just drapery and folds, in a word, painting"—that served to emphasize the canvas's sensuality in a subliminal way: for example, the corners of a pillow sticking up toward a "a fine, dark crease in a red fabric," and "the great swath of red velvet hanging down on the left ...[is] a metaphor of the male sex."[2]

Fragonard has his frivolous side, too, because he expresses his libertine themes both in a relatively classic style, as here, and with the profuse decorativeness of the rococo or rocaille style (two related terms that refer, in painting, to more or less the same baroque inspiration), which became

ABOVE
JOHANN JOSEPH ZOFFANY
(1733–1810), *Queen Charlotte with Her
Two Eldest Sons*, c. 1765. The painting
depicts the Queen of England
at her dressing table with a longcase
equation clock in the background.
Royal Collection Trust, London.

FACING PAGE
Ferdinand Berthoud (1727–1807),
LONGCASE EQUATION CLOCK,
c. 1750. This exceptional clock is
typical of the Regency style.
The dial is by Julien II Le Roy,
the cabinet by Charles Cressent.
Royal Collection Trust, London.

fashionable in the 1730s. He does this in masterly fashion in another famous painting, his charmingly bawdy *The Swing*, commissioned by an aristocrat who requested that he himself be depicted in the figure getting an unexpected glimpse beneath his mistress's skirts, as they billow up with the movement of the swing— pushed by … a bishop. Here Fragonard perfectly follows the teaching of his master, François Boucher, the most famous of the rocaille painters at the time. This style was well defined by the austere Diderot, in 1761, criticizing the painter's "mannerisms": "His elegance, his affected winsomeness, his novelistic gallantry, his coquetry, his taste, his facility, variety, brilliancy, his made-up complexions, his debauchery, necessarily captivate fops, little women, young men, society people, the crowd of those who are strangers to real taste, to the truth, to just ideas, and to the seriousness of art."[3] There is nothing serious, indeed, about this profusion of details, flowers and branches, soft and bright hues, bared pink flesh, which, thanks to the painter's dazzling technique, create charming tableaux of a certain lifestyle. Antoine Watteau was the precursor of this style, which was illustrated during the century by other great painters such as Quentin de La Tour, Élisabeth Vigée Le Brun, and Thomas Gainsborough.

The same "affected winsomeness" was applied to the furniture and objets d'arts which filled fashionable salons, as well as to gold- and silverwork, as we have seen in the rose watch chain described above. The rococo style added a touch of fantasy to furniture, notably in bronze ornamentation such as foliage, ribbons, and winged figures, or polychrome

motifs with inlaid ivory or coral, and fine marquetry. New types of furniture made their appearance, also reflecting a desire for comfort—the chest of drawers, the dressing-table, the writing desk—and the pleasures of society amusements, with the game or card table. Attractively decorated snuffboxes, needlework boxes, and candy boxes abounded and were part of the decor. Goldsmiths and ceramicists used their imagination to create lavishly decorated tableware: a lid with a handle in the shape of an animal; a salt cellar, like the one made for the king of Portugal by the goldsmith Thomas Germain, in the shape of a shell supported by two fish. Dining tables were laid with fine porcelain from the great European factories, particularly Meissen in Saxony, which kept its trade secret—the use of kaolin—until 1768, and Sèvres in France. In Sèvres, the porcelain's rocaille motifs were designed by François Boucher and Jean-Claude Duplessis, père. And among all these precious objects and furniture designs, rococo "chinoiseries," which also appear in painting and in sculpture, were particularly popular at the time.

Naturally, neither women's nor men's fashions escaped this trend. A type of gown known as a "robe à la française," characterized by its box pleats at the back, appeared circa 1730 and was popular throughout Europe. It was usually made of silk, embroidered or woven with large, sinuous motifs in bright colors that sometimes matched the decoration of a watch and chain worn at the waist. Marie-Antoinette, who adored fashion and had no fear of eccentricity, followed the advice of Rose Bertin, her "minister of fashions," and wore elaborate, high

hair styles created by her hairdresser, Léonard. Her court gowns in brocade, damask, lampas, or silk velvet were embroidered with gold and silver thread, but she was also fond of simple country-style dresses in chiffon to play the farmer's wife at her hamlet in the park at Versailles.

The rococo men's coat also took on a more eye-catching, fancy look, although it made the wearer look somewhat affected, a little too elegant, and earned him the nickname of *petit marquis*. Such coats were made of a range of materials: "speckled, striped, floral, leafy, 'vermicellied,' and silver-spangled fabrics, with countless splashes and shades of color,"[4] embellished with precious embroidery and fancy buttons.

In France, this decorative proliferation in the arts, furniture, and clothing was hardly to be found in architecture, except in certain country or garden follies—often fanciful and extravagant imitations of Greco-Roman or exotic styles—where all sorts of goings-on were tolerated. The great French architect of this century, Ange-Jacques Gabriel, "first architect to the king" Louis XV, who designed the Château de Compiègne, the Petit Trianon, and the Opéra Royal at Versailles, rigorously cultivated the classical rules of architecture. The only notable exception being, in the new interiors of French homes, the replacement of long rows of rooms with more intimate, comfortable, and better heated spaces propitious for conversation. Rococo in architecture, the last variation of baroque, was far more in evidence in Austria and Germany, Bohemia, Italy, and Spain. One of the most charming examples of a large rococo residence is the summer palace of Frederick II of Prussia—Frederick the Great—Sanssouci, near Potsdam. It was completed in 1747, and Voltaire, who was living in Potsdam at the time, was often a guest there between 1750 and 1753. On a vine-carpeted slope, the architect Georg Wenzeslaus von Knobelsdorff built, in accordance with the king's detailed instructions, a row of ten rooms on a single level. Facing the vineyards, the yellow façade, with large windows along its length and an elegant rounded central pavilion, was decorated with rococo atlantes and caryatids in the form of maenads, the female followers of Dionysus, the Greek god of wine and drunken revelry. The successors of Frederick the Great accentuated the rococo style of the estate even further, with the addition of chinoiserie decors and follies.

Madame de Pompadour also had her own rocaille home, the Château de Bellevue in Meudon, built for her at great expense by her favorite architect, Jean Cailleteau, known as "Lassurance." The interior of this square, two-story building was filled with the decorative elements she favored: carved woodwork featuring hunting and fishing cherubs by Jacques Verberckt, decorative panels by the animal painter Jean-Baptiste Oudry, trumeaux and fantasy or "Turkish" paintings by Carle Van Loo, rococo paintings including chinoiseries by François Boucher, and so on. But the luminaries of the Enlightenment would soon fade, and with them, the frivolities of a lifestyle far removed from the extreme rigors suffered by the starving masses: Madame de Pompadour's chateau was demolished and its contents dispersed after the Revolution. ⌛

WATCHMAKING
FROM 1715 TO 1795

The period of the Lumières, or Enlightenment, was the second golden age of French clockmaking, lasting until the 1850s. England, which was at the cutting edge of technology, had its own golden age between 1650 and 1750, but could not rival the flawless aesthetics of the timepieces made in Paris.

According to Ferdinand Berthoud, the profession of clockmaker can be divided into the craftsman who practices his discipline "without the first notion of it" and "the mechanic-architect, an artist who embraces this science as a whole," and who therefore has broad-ranging knowledge in the field. Clock production itself can be divided into three categories. Spits, traditional features in large kitchens since the fifteenth century, belfry and turret clocks, and chiming mechanisms were forged by blacksmith-clockmakers. Interior timepieces were the specialty of clockmakers, and watches by watchmakers, who produced a small volume of pieces. Notions dealers, wholesalers, and jewelers bought and sold luxury objects including clocks and watches and, in anticipating fashion trends, influenced their designs.

The elite developed a passion for the sciences. At Versailles, the king was interested in the most sophisticated mechanisms and their cases, works of art in their own right. Parisian mansions were home to numerous timepieces, just like the royal palaces. French taste was imitated and spread throughout Europe.

In the seventeenth century, the pendulum clock served more as a decorative object than a measuring instrument. A period of transition followed, during which asymmetrical designs and rocaille became popular. Both flourished in the Louis XV style, in which bronze predominated. Works by Jacques and Philippe II Caffieri père and fils, Charles Cressent, Jean-Claude Duplessis, François-Thomas Germain, Jean-Joseph de Saint-Germain, and Robert Osmond are among the best known of the period. The original bronze casts were so valuable that they were included in the capital stock of workshops and sold when a business went bankrupt or terminated its activity. Bronze decorations of branches dotted with birds, fauns, or mythological divinities contrasted with the tinted horn or dark wood of decorative wall clocks and enhanced the shape of rosewood floor clocks. All-bronze wall clocks might feature a Diana, or, reflecting the vogue for the Far East and exoticism, a fanciful Chinese figure. Animal

FACING PAGE
THE CREATION OF THE WORLD clock, 1754, by François-Thomas Germain (1726–1791), silversmith and sculptor; Claude-Siméon Passemant (1702–1769), engineer; and Joseph-Léonard Roque, clockmaker. This masterpiece has recently been restored by Vacheron Constantin, the musée du Louvre and the Atelier Chronos. Musée du Louvre, Paris.

BELOW
Louis XV ASTRONOMICAL CLOCK, 1749–53, by Louis Dauthiau, Jacques and Philippe Caffieri, and Claude-Siméon Passemant. Amongst other indications, the clock displays true and average time, an annual calendar, day and month taking into account leap years, millennial years until 9999, phases and eclipses of the moon, and, within the crystal sphere on top, the movement of the planets. Château de Versailles.

clocks, the fashion for which was without precedent, were supported by a camel, an elephant, a lion, or a rhinoceros, or else a wild boar or a bull, generally in bronze with a dark patina. The animal sat on a gilt bronze rocaille support, sometimes set on a base containing a chime mechanism. However, these flawless decorations embellishing clocks with beautifully crafted movements were rivaled by certain unparalleled technological masterpieces. The astronomical clock with bronzes sculpted by Jacques Caffieri and Philippe Caffieri, fils, showed apparent or true time and solar time, calendar indications calculated until 9999, and phases and eclipses of the moon. The crystal sphere at the top showed the planets in motion. "The Creation of the World" clock featured, in an astonishingly modern gilt bronze and silver setting, a precision planisphere, the lunar phases with a revolving globe, and a sphere with rising and descending poles to indicate the different lengths of the day according to the season. These two works designed by the engineer Claude-Siméon Passemant created such a sensation that identical replicas were reproduced a century later on the request of several wealthy collectors.

The eighteenth century was also the time of automata. Although artificial, these were true to life down to their smallest details. With his flute player, tambourine player, and duck, Jacques de Vaucanson sought to achieve "a reproduction in view of obtaining the experimental intelligence of a biological mechanism." He was imitated notably in Switzerland, by Frédéric Leschot and by Henri Maillardet, and, in Austria, by Frederik von Klaus, who built several writing automata. Pierre Jaquet-Droz and his son Henri-Louis made use of Swiss clockmaking expertise to produce remarkable automata including a writer, a draftsman, a musician, and many singing birds. Mechanical paintings, which appeared at Versailles during the reign of Louis XIV, had become popular as a source of entertainment and among science enthusiasts. Their mechanisms brought to life small scenes peopled with dozens of figures, in a landscape with architectural features inspired by the French School of painting. After 1796, the year the device was invented by the Swiss Antoine Favre, these mechanical paintings would come with a musical box.

The first architectural excavations at Pompeii reflected a renewed interest in the ancient world. With its simple, graceful lines, the Louis XVI style embraced new designs: clocks would take the form of an urn, or vase, a boundary stone (with an arched top), or a temple. German, Austrian, and American clockmakers adopted clock designs with themes and figures drawn from mythology, current affairs, or that celebrated the arts and sciences. Skeleton pendulum clocks with visible mechanisms were produced in most European countries. The precision regulator

designed to stand on a piece of furniture, either a simple model or an astronomical clock, was developed by renowned clockmakers including Berthoud, Breguet, Janvier, Lepaute, and Robin.

In the eighteenth century, the watch was an important decorative accessory for men and women alike. To catch the eye, it was worn at the end of a chain attached to a belt. Whether made in Paris or in Geneva, it was a particularly elegant object and reflected the taste for painting on enamel. In the early decades, rocaille motifs framed enameled scenes in the taste of fashionable painters, soon to be replaced by bucolic or classical themes. The English watch differed from its continental counterparts in its double or even triple case, the use of painted horn, and rare use of painting on enamel. Pieces produced for Eastern markets featured semiprecious or precious stones and enameled scenes. Between 1750 and 1850, Switzerland gained an unparalleled reputation in the art of painting on enamel, using the patented "sous-fondant" technique developed by their master craftsmen.

Once the consequences of the revocation of the Edict of Nantes had stabilized, Paris regained an enviable reputation, attracting clockmaking personalities from abroad such as Ferdinand Berthoud, Abraham-Louis Breguet, and Jean Romilly. Huygen's inventions had shed light on the influence of temperature and atmospheric pressure, bringing about improvements in accuracy. Research in this field continued throughout the century, pioneered by English and expatriate clockmakers in London, resulting in the dead-beat anchor escapement and the cylinder escapement for use in watches, and in the compensation pendulum (George Graham), the detached escapement for watches (Thomas Mudge), and the detent escapement (Pierre Le Roy). Jean Romilly developed the dead-second watch with a central hand that jumped at each second; Jean-Moïse Pouzait invented the watch with an independent seconds train, the precursor of the chronograph. Pierre Augustin Caron, famous in the literary world under the name of Beaumarchais, created a keyless winding timepiece for Madame de Pompadour. Sarton, Perrelet, and Breguet contributed to the development of the self-winding watch. Le Plat and Cox made the first clocks powered by variations in atmospheric pressure. After a hard-fought battle between Pierre Le Roy, Ferdinand Berthoud, and others, John Harrison discovered the solution to the problem of longitudes. Julien Le Roy's horizontal or flat-bed turret clock, the Lépine caliber for watches, and the significant headway made by Breguet, opened the way for clock- and watchmaking in the nineteenth century. **D.F.**

THE TIME OF
MODERNITY

On October 14, 1815—the day Napoleon, prisoner of the English, arrived at Saint Helena after an Atlantic crossing lasting over two months—in Paris, Casimir de Montrond entered the Breguet clockmaker's shop on the Quai de l'Horloge, near the Pont Neuf. The founder of the firm, Abraham-Louis Breguet, was aged seventy and still working, with his son Antoine-Louis. Breguet was one of the great clockmakers of his time: among other major innovations, he had invented the automatic watch, the gong-spring, and the tourbillon. But he had also popularized a style of watch: an extremely elegant casing, with an original yet understated design. His guilloché dials and thin "apple" hands had become classics. One of his designs featuring an off-center hour dial had been very popular for the last three years. And it was precisely this model that the comte de Montrond wished to purchase. The man was famous in Paris for his elegance (he was compared to Beau Brummell), his wit, womanizing, and gambling, his fortune made on the stock exchange, and especially, his friendship with the prince de Talleyrand, for whom he had carried out delicate missions for twenty years. He chose this watch not only for its off-center dial, but also because it was extra-thin and would not make a bump in the pocket of his waistcoat. The model he selected had a guilloché gold case, a silver guilloché dial, and an hour dial in appliqué silver. The hours were in Roman numerals and the hands in the "apple" style. On one side of the dial was a fast-slow indicator; on the other, the signature "Breguet & Fils" in an appliqué oval. And above, an openwork aperture indicated the phases of the moon on midnight blue enamel. This watch, just ten millimeters thick, remains timelessly beautiful in its spare design.

This watch is today among the treasures of the Beyer Clock and Watch Museum in Zurich. With a few others from the same period, it represents the emergence, in the latter years of the eighteenth century, of the modern men's watch: modern not only in its movement, but also in its pared-down style. It was a style that followed on from neoclassicism and flourished in France under the First Empire. A style, also, that corresponded to the new norms of male elegance established in England and embodied by the most famous of dandies, George Brummell. Born in 1778 in London into a well-to-do family that provided him with an excellent education, George "Beau" Brummell was noticed for his charm and wit by the Prince of Wales, the future George IV, when he was just eighteen years old. At the age of twenty-one he inherited a small fortune, and quickly became the darling of London society, which was fascinated by his own brand of elegance. Measured with absolute precision in order to go unnoticed, achieving a level of perfection that made it almost invisible, Brummell's style was anything but ostentatious: black tailcoat, fawn waistcoat, and suede trousers or breeches for daywear; and for the evening, dark blue coat, white waistcoat, white necktie, pantaloons, silk stockings, and pumps. To this rigorously low-key look, Brummell added impeccable cleanliness of person and clothing, and daily shaving. "Such unflagging moderation bordered on the invisible," writes Farid Chenoune, "yet was so

FACING PAGE
BREGUET EXTRA-THIN SIMPLE POCKET WATCH, 1815, Paris. Engine-turned gold case with engine-turned silver dial signed "Breguet & Fils". Off-center applied silver annular hour and minute dial. Moon phases on enamel by aperture with age of the moon sector. Fast/slow sector. Extra-thin movement engraved "N° 2686 Breguet". Beyer Zurich Clock and Watch Museum.

———

ABOVE
EUGÈNE DELACROIX (1798–1863) *Portrait of Louis-Auguste Schwiter*, 1826–30. A close friend of Delacroix, Schwiter (1805–1889) was a Romantic painter celebrated for his portraits and landscapes. The National Gallery, London.

spectacular that Brummell's contemporaries were awed; this stimulating and paralyzing paradox made it impossible to imitate him, since there was nothing to copy."[1]

Brummell nevertheless inspired the dark and austere modern men's suit, which endures today in all formal contexts and among white-collar workers, and that can only be brightened up with a tie. The French Anglomania, which at the turn of the nineteenth century was nothing new, only hastened the spread of this model on the continent, where Brummell became a legend, especially in France. Despite his fame, he died in Caen in 1840 in impoverished circumstances, ruined by gambling debts, but Balzac had already immortalized him in his *Traité de la vie élégante* (Treatise on Elegant Living) published ten years earlier in five articles that appeared in the journal *La Mode*. In it, he refers frequently to Brummell, as someone who had understood that supreme elegance was not to distinguish oneself: "If people scrutinize the way you look, you are not well dressed: you are too well dressed, too stiff, you are trying too hard." Having understood this, Brummell would spend hours every day achieving it. Dandyism would later appear in many of the characters in Balzac's *Human Comedy*, such as Lucien de Rubempré and Henri de Marsay.

This elegance of this understated manner of dress, which emerged as a manifestation of modernity at the time, followed on naturally from neoclassicism. The style appeared in the arts in the second half of the eighteenth century, as both a reaction to the artificiality of rococo and a quest for a kind of simplicity seen as a return to the roots of antiquity, a virtue, sometimes the dream of a better world. The prints of the Rome-based Venetian artist Piranesi, inspired by classical Rome, the discovery of Herculaneum, and the excavations of the ancient city, which brought treasures to light throughout this half-century, played an important role in this return to the ancient canons of beauty, which also fueled dreams and a model of harmony for the future. In architecture, this lay behind the work of the likes of Claude Nicolas Ledoux, a proponent of the pure geometric form; among his buildings still standing today, besides numerous drawings, are the Hôtel d'Hallwyll and the Rotonde de la Villette tollhouse in Paris, the Château de Bénouville in Normandy, and several buildings of the Royal Saltworks at Arc-et-Senans in the Doubs in eastern France. A taste for architecture of the Doric order also developed in the same period and in the same spirit, as illustrated in Germany, for example, by David Gilly and his son Friedrich, as did Palladianism in England and in France, and a Greek Revival movement, mostly in England. In sculpture, this trend mostly flourished in Italy, with the master Antonio Canova, who combined free inspiration and classical conventions, and the Danish sculptor Bertel Thorvaldsen, more radical in his respect of traditions, who lived and worked mostly in Rome. Numerous European artists of every discipline gravitated naturally to Rome, either during their Grand Tour, which took them inevitably to Italy, or for an almost obligatory study trip. Ingres was among them: five years after winning the Prix de Rome scholarship, he discovered the city in 1806,

ABOVE

CHARLES PERCIER (1764–1838), *View of a Roman house*, 1797. This former resident of Palazzo Mancini in Rome became the official architect of Napoleon Bonaparte, with his friend and associate Pierre Fontaine (1762–1853). Together, they invented the Empire style.

FACING PAGE

MANTEL CLOCK, c. 1813, after a project by Charles Percier. The Sèvres biscuit case is in the form of an antique altar dedicated to the sun; the pedestal represents the four seasons. Cité de la céramique, Sèvres.

at the age of twenty-six, and stayed for many years. Along with Jacques-Louis David—who arrived in Rome in the same context and at the same age, but almost thirty years earlier (he painted his famous *Oath of the Horatii* there)—Ingres became the French neoclassical painter par excellence, employing a good deal of freedom in his academicism: "High society folks," wrote Baudelaire in 1855, "were impressed by M. Ingres on account of his pompous love of antiquity and of tradition. To the eccentrics and to the blasé, to the host of the over-fastidious always in search of novelty, even it if is bitter, he appealed by his strangeness."[2]

Neoclassicism became the official art of Napoleon I, who asked painters to forgo the ancient world and glorify his own exploits. The emperor imposed the genre not only in France but also in conquered Europe, notably through the decorative arts where the Empire style flourished everywhere. In French palaces, such as Fontainebleau and Rambouillet, and in those of Antwerp, Amsterdam, Florence, and Turin, the precepts established by the French architects Charles Percier and Pierre François Léonard Fontaine, in their *Recueil de décorations intérieures* (Collection of Interior Designs), were methodically applied. A somewhat martial concern for rationality favored by the emperor brought a concern for symmetry, the straight line, and imposing volumes to furniture and decoration—characteristics more often associated with architectural structures. But this did not prevent a certain gracefulness in the gilt bronze wall lamps with classical and mythological motifs produced in the workshops of the bronze caster Pierre-Philippe Thomire, and which sometimes adorned the furniture of the great cabinetmaker of the time, Jacob-Desmalter. Nor did it prevent the wave of Egyptomania—on Napoleon's return from the Egyptian campaign—which inspired the decoration of furniture and tableware.

In 1815, after Napoleon's abdication, the outcome of the Empire was in many ways tragic. The Napoleonic Wars had devastated continental Europe, with the cost in human life estimated at a million deaths in France and three million throughout Europe. The wars had left France in ruin: the country had lost Savoy, Belgium, and the left bank of the Rhine—Revolutionary conquests—and its colonial possessions, including Louisiana, which was sold to the United States. On an economic level, the country's situation was disastrous: both its debt and the war reparations to be paid to the allies were colossal. And yet it was thanks to Napoleon that France had become a modern and united nation. While the Empire had flouted the Revolutionary ideal of liberty, it had strengthened notions of equality, merit-based promotion, and property rights, and had created institutions and legislation that were so solid that nothing has durably shaken them since: the Conseil d'État, the Sénat, the Code Civil. The emperor also created a competent and impartial administration, and facilitated enterprise, effective finance, and industrial innovation that was presented at the Expositions des Produits de l'Industrie Française, predecessors of the World's Fairs. Furthermore, the Napoleonic era forged a new international spirit: before long,

FACING PAGE
An Empire gilt and patinated bronze and rouge griotte marble "À L'ÉGYPTIENNE" CLOCK, c. 1805, Paris. Eight-day duration movement by Mesnil à Paris, housed in a case by André-Antoine Ravrio (1759–1814) after a design by Thomas Hope (1769–1831). Richard Redding Antiques, Switzerland.

ABOVE
GIOVANNI BATTISTA PIRANESI (1720–1778), Egyptian-style fireplace, 1769. Engraving from the series entitled *Diverse maniere d'adornare i cammini* (Different ways to adorn a fireplace). Gabinetto Comunale delle Stampe, Rome.

PAGE 136
View of a part of the library in the HÔTEL DE BEAUHARNAIS, 1714, in Paris, a particularly representative masterpiece of Empire style that introduced symmetry into furniture and decoration, adorned with gilt bronze antique motifs.

PAGE 137
JACQUES-LOUIS DAVID (1748–1825), *Napoleon in His Study* (detail), 1812. This portrait shows the Emperor Napoleon I wearing the uniform of an officer in his study in the Tuileries. In the right background, there is an Empire-style clock. National Gallery of Art, Washington.

from London to Moscow, merchants, intellectuals, and artists, fascinated by the grandeur of the imperial vision, were building upon its ruins a semblance of the Europe of which Napoleon had dreamed.

The Napoleonic myth of a multifaceted genius who was master of the world and yet outlawed, naturally fueled the Romanticism that had been flourishing in the arts since the late eighteenth century. Toward 1827, as he was penning the preface to his play *Cromwell*, a romantic manifesto against the three unities of classical drama, Victor Hugo publicly declared his support for the Napoleonic ideal and composed his ode *À la Colonne de la place Vendôme* (To the Place Vendôme Column)—the column in question a monument erected between 1807 and 1810 by the emperor to commemorate his own glory. In his collection of poems *Les Châtiments*, published in 1852, Hugo endowed Napoleon with mythical status in his long poem *L'Expiation*. The iconic emperor also marked the works of Stendhal and Balzac.

All of the arts became steeped in Romanticism in the first part of the nineteenth century, following the *Sturm und Drang* literary movement born in Germany in the 1770s, of which the young Goethe—who would later become a fervent supporter of Napoleon—was part. The *Athenaeum* journal was founded in 1798 by the brothers August Wilhelm and Friedrich Schlegel in Berlin as a reaction against classicism and reason and in defense of the irrational, mystical, and sentimental in art; among its most famous contributors was the poet Novalis. Jean-Jacques Rousseau in France, Edmund Burke in England, and Johann Gottlieb

Fichte in Germany would also have considerable influence on the Romantic movement, which advocated freedom of inspiration, the exaltation of sentiment and passion, the expression of the violence of desire, of the power of love and death, of melancholy, of revolt, and of dreams. From the late 1810s, an English poet was inspiring all of Romantic Europe: Lord Byron, following the extraordinary success of his four-part poem *Childe Harold's Pilgrimage*, published between 1812 and 1818. But his dandyism, his pose as a solitary and melancholic traveler, his support for Greek independence, and his heroic death did more for Byronism than his work.

The Romantic inspiration also permeated music, which was undergoing a period of considerable development, with the invention of the modern piano circa 1820, musical performance being increasingly valued for its own sake, symphonic orchestration becoming more elaborate, and opera more popular. Following Ludwig van Beethoven—and before Giuseppe Verdi—Frédéric Chopin, Hector Berlioz, and Robert Schumann were some of the great musical figures of the time.

With this new cult of the self, of inspiration as guide, and of the subject as a reflection of the soul, the Romantic painters brought a great variety of new images that shook up painterly conventions and established a different kind of modernity. This can be seen in the light- and color-drenched landscapes of the German Caspar David Friedrich and in those of the English painter J.M.W. Turner, both of whom would inspire the Impressionists in the latter part of the century. But Romanticism in

painting reached its height in France especially, where the neoclassical tradition of the likes of David was reinterpreted, in the late eighteenth century, by painters such as Anne-Louis Girodet. Girodet's mythic *The Sleep of Endymion* depicted a languorous ephebe caressed by a ray of moonlight, and drew the admiration of Chateaubriand and Balzac. The neoclassical influence is still clearly evident in Théodore Géricault's grandiose masterpiece *The Raft of the Medusa*, first shown in Paris at the 1819 Salon Officiel of the Académie des Beaux Arts—as if the artist's newfound freedom could only flourish in subverting convention. Inspired by a recent tragedy—the shipwreck three years earlier of the frigate *Méduse* off the coast of Africa, which led to the castaways resorting to cannibalism— the monumental painting (approximately 16 ½ × 23 ft./5 × 7 m) said more about the morbid fascination of the painter than about the real suffering of the survivors. Géricault went to the extent of having some of them pose for him, and retrieved body parts from morgues to study in his studio. Despite the depiction of muscular nudes in the style of neoclassical painting, the extremely dramatic composition of intertwined, exhausted survivors and corpses, livid horror, and final hope in a crepuscular light, violently sweeps away the stiff lifelessness of the classical allegories. The work met with mixed success at the Salon, but was admired by a crowd of some forty thousand people the following year in London.

The Raft of the Medusa greatly impressed a young painter aged twenty, Eugène Delacroix. He would go on to become the most eclectic, prolific, and complete French Romantic painter. His first success at the Salon was in 1822 with his *The Barque of Dante*, whose allegorical theme, dramatic composition, chiaroscuro, light and shade, livid bodies, torment, and strong contrasts evoked, and equaled, the masterpiece of his elder. He explored the same allegorical vein eight years later in one of his most famous paintings, this time with a political connotation, *Liberty Leading the People*. In the meantime, Delacroix had added to his Romantic palette the bright and colorful emotions of a form of orientalism that had already been cultivated by Victor Hugo and Lord Byron, and which he developed during a journey to North Africa in 1832. He brought seven sketchbooks back from his trip, which led to more than eighty paintings. Far from succumbing to the picturesque, they show how much of a revelation this journey was for the painter, who had been dazzled, as he wrote in a letter, by the "striking sublimity that lies all about one here, and staggers one with its reality,"[3] and especially—and it was decisive for the rest of his work—by the "rare and precious influence of the sun which gives an intense life to everything." It was a real sun that shone through his painting, which would influence all the Impressionists and prompt Baudelaire to say of Delacroix that he was "the first of the Moderns." ⧗

FACING PAGE
THÉODORE GÉRICAULT (1791–1824), *The Charging Chasseur*, 1812. Painted in a neoclassical style, this equestrian portrait recalls David's famous *Bonaparte Crossing the Great Saint Bernard Pass*. Musée du Louvre, Paris.

ABOVE
Jean-Simon Deverberie (1764–1824), Directoire gilt bronze **CHARIOT CLOCK** of eight-day duration, c. 1800, Paris. Arabic numerals and blue steel Breguet hands for the hours and minutes set within the wheel of a chariot, which is cast at center with twelve foliate and fluted spokes set at five-minute intervals. Richard Redding Antiques, Switzerland.

WATCHMAKING FROM 1795 TO 1850

The growing demand in the eighteenth century for a thinner timepiece prompted Jean-Antoine Lépine to reinvent the architecture of the watch mechanism. In a series of stages, the Lépine caliber, the structure of which is still used today, was born. Because of its thinness, the watchmaker also redesigned the characteristics of the case, which probably makes Lépine the first to explore the aesthetic possibilities of a watch.

Academies played a significant role in facilitating communication between the British, French, and Swiss watchmakers and enabling them to share their inventions, which were seen as contributing not only to progress in the sciences but also in modern life in general. The inventions contributed by Abraham-Louis Breguet included, for the watch, a self-winding mechanism, an anti-shock device, the tourbillon, and improvements to Thomas Mudge's perpetual calendar of the early 1760s. The constant force escapement, a mechanism for stopping the second hand, a forerunner of the split-seconds chronoscope, and the double barrel provided improvements to chronometers and precision regulators. Breguet's technical as well as aesthetic investigations influenced the whole of the watch- and clockmaking world in the first half of the nineteenth century. This period also saw research into the measurement of short time intervals and even fractions of a second. To meet the needs of astronomers, Louis Moinet built a chronoscope capable of measuring 1/60th of a second that he named a *compteur de tierces*. Shortly afterward, Nicolas Mathieu Rieussec in France and Frederick Louis Fatton in England patented inking chronographs for horse breeders, among others. Numerous inventions followed, culminating in that of a chronograph for industry and the medical world in the second half of the century.

Napoleon's military campaigns fueled the taste for Roman antiquities and inspired a fashion for Egyptian art. These trends influenced the Directoire style, a period of transition between the Louis XV and Empire styles. The pre-Romantic movement of the time also gave rise to popular literary works portraying the luxuriant beauty of tropical flora and fauna. The notion of the "noble savage" was reflected in the decorative arts: bronze work and more specifically clocks featured depictions of native Americans or African figures as imagined by Europeans at the time, shown either in an African context or as enslaved people in America. Jean-Simon Deverberie was the first bronze caster to patent the basic models, including the figures

ABOVE
"PALLAS ATHENA" CLOCK, c. 1820,
Paris. Gilt and patinated bronze,
and red marble, case attributed
to Gérard-Jean Galle (1788–1846).
The case depicts the standing figure
of the goddess wearing a plumed
helmet and laurel wreath, as well as
a short tunic beneath a long cloak
gathered at the shoulder. Richard
Redding Antiques, Switzerland.

———

FACING PAGE
Zacharie Raingo, Empire gilt bronze
mounted amboyna **ORRERY CLOCK**,
c. 1815, Paris. The orrery of four-year
duration consists of rotating spheres
representing the sun, earth, and moon,
with an ivory handle below for manual
operation, the pillars supported on
a circular trellis-cast gilt bronze base.
Richard Redding Antiques, Switzerland.

of Africa and America personified as two female hunters, symbolized by a tortoise and a lion for the first, and an alligator and a palm tree for the second. Among these clocks produced between 1795 to 1825, the rarest model by Deverberie is a bust of an African women with a feather headdress and pleated tunic, whose eyes display the hours and minutes.

The "noble savage" clock heralded designs in the Romantic style that developed after the return of historicism, with motifs evoking the Middle Ages, Henri IV, Napoleon on Saint Helena, and Mary Stuart. Another Romantic theme—that of the ennobling of the common laborer—was seen in clocks known as "*les petits métiers*" (the small trades): sailor, oyster carrier, gardener, water seller, blacksmith, or butterfly catcher, and many others, were executed in an elegant, idealized manner.

The majestic and imposing Empire style made new use of symmetry and disregarded nature. Its perfectly carved decorative motifs—the Sphinx, the Gorgon, spread eagles, caryatids, and military emblems—were borrowed from ancient art and Greco-Roman poetry. A chariot with the dial set in the wheel or a columned clock topped with a pediment or an arch were the most popular models. Bronze and marble, alone or in combination, alabaster, crystal, and wood were the most often used materials.

Astronomical clocks continued to be made, following on from the designs of the Enlightenment but benefiting from recent discoveries. The indisputable master in this period was Antide Janvier, who was active under the monarchy, the Empire, and the Restoration. His masterpiece was shown at the 1801 Exposition des Produits de l'Industrie Française, and was universally hailed by the scientific world. It indicated the periods of all of the planets in the solar system, including Uranus, which had been discovered in 1781.

In 1842, Jean-Baptiste Schwilgué completed the mechanisms of Strasbourg Cathedral's third clock, in which he installed a perpetual calendar of his own design and that took account of the secular years of the Gregorian calendar. Among the complications of this major work were solar and lunar equations, a celestial globe with a rotation of approximately 25,800 years, a planetary dial, and an ecclesiastic and civil calendar.

In terms of the aesthetics of the watch, the innovations of Abraham-Louis Breguet were significant enough to establish a Breguet style. A smooth or delicately guillochéd back and middle enhanced the pure lines of an extra-thin case. Enameled dials with Arabic numerals and "apple" hands were designed to be easy to read. At the same time, Breguet created a new kind of dial featuring Roman numerals engraved on a gold or silver ring. The vacant central space could accommodate various apertures or mini-dials, according to the watch's functions.

Fancy watches were, in contrast to the designs of Lépine and Breguet, a return to the fashions of the sixteenth century. A specialty of Geneva and also Vienna, the bee, cricket, or beetle replaced the rabbit, dog, or lion. Camellia, rose, and peony, mango, or cherry were enameled in realistic colors. A miniature harp, mandolin, or violin were additional choices of motif for these precious and decorative objects. **D.F.**

FACING PAGE
Antide Janvier (1751–1835), **TABLE REGULATOR** of eight-day duration, 1781, Paris. Mahogany case with oval blue and white Sèvres biscuit plaques to either side. Though this ingenious regulator was made before the Revolution, it bears the date of 1781, which relates to the death of Thomas Morel, who commissioned the work. Below the first dial is an added silvered plaque, covering Janvier's original signature; its Latin inscription translates "He passed onto a better life. 4th May 1797." Richard Redding Antiques, Switzerland.

————
BELOW
PENDANT WATCH IN THE FORM OF A VIOLIN containing a receptacle for scent, c. 1830. The case covered with a translucent red enamel on guilloché ground, decorated with a musical score on a lectern comprising an engraved branch, highlighted with green champlevé enamel flowers. Musée international d'horlogerie, La Chaux-de-Fonds.

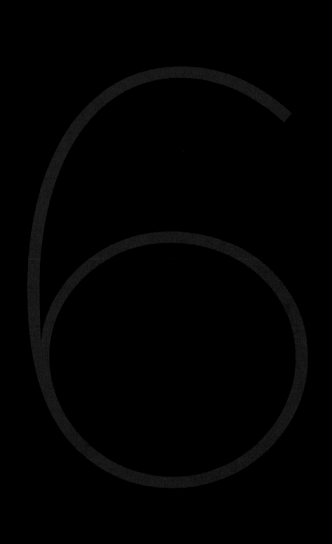

THE TIME OF
INDUSTRY AND ENTERPRISE

At the Paris Exposition Universelle of 1855, the famous bronzeworks Delafontaine, a firm headed at the time by the grandson of the founder, Auguste-Maximilien, exhibited some of its precious decorative objects and art works. Among them was an Eastern-inspired "Persian" clock. It had been executed after a drawing by the sculptor Geoffroy-Dechaume, who was particularly talented in designing gold and silver work and went on to specialize in medieval art. He contributed notably to the neo-Gothic restoration of Paris's Notre-Dame Cathedral, under the supervision of Viollet-le-Duc. Made of gilded and silver-gilt bronze, the clock was an example of the eclecticism pervading the decorative arts and architecture during the second half of the nineteenth century: artists drew inspiration from the forms and ornamentations of the past, or from foreign lands, and mixed them to create a new aesthetic. This object resembles something from an exotic dream rather than taking its inspiration from an actual decorative style: its sophisticated decoration features an odd blend of Chinese motifs—bronze feet on a marble base, two dragons flanking the dial—Perso-Arabic references with the Eastern Arabic numerals for the hours and the engravings on the dial, and a sort of Eastern baroque style for the bronze crown of carved arabesques at the top.

Charles Baudelaire was a friend of Geoffroy-Dechaume (in 2013, one of the five known self-portraits of the poet were discovered among the painter's archives), but it is not known if he saw this clock. An art critic and an ever-curious observer, he visited the Exposition of 1855 and wrote a review of the show, which was published in a posthumous collection of some of his writings on art, *Curiosités esthétiques*. "There can be few occupations more interesting, more absorbing, so full of surprises and revelations, than comparison between nations and their respective products."[1]

Regarding a decorative object from a distant country, China, he explains: "This object is a sample of universal beauty; but if it is to be understood, the critic, the viewer, must bring about within himself a transformation, which is something of a mystery, and, by a phenomenon of will-power acting on his imagination, he must learn by his own effort to share in the life of the society that has given birth to this unexpected bloom … this whole world of new harmonies will slowly enter into him, penetrate him patiently like the steam of a scented bath house; all these unknown springs of life will be added to his own."[2]

An exoticism of "new harmonies" that would heighten the viewer's own vitality ("springs of life"): this was a far cry indeed from a Romantic orientalism steeped in nostalgia for antiquity. Knowledge of Eastern harmonies (exoticism at the time being limited to the Near and Far East) would broaden horizons of knowledge, and foster and enrich a creativity that looked to the future. And so, in the second half of the nineteenth century, orientalist painters rejected sentiment and emotion, devoting themselves instead to the objective, realistic depiction of the faces, costumes, decors, and landscapes of the countries they visited. Among the most famous of them, Jean-Léon Gérôme, Eugène Fromentin, and John Frederick

Lewis shared an ethnographical concern to show what was "true" and make it known and appealing to the world. They were encouraged in their work by the first travel photographers, including the writer Maxime Du Camp, who, with his calotype camera, accompanied Flaubert on his Middle Eastern journey between 1848 and 1852.

In a similar spirit of knowledge, of encyclopedic scope this time, the British architect and interior designer Owen Jones—one of the Superintendents of Works for the Great Exhibition of 1851 in London—published his extraordinary *Grammar of Ornament* in 1856. It included a hundred or so color plates presenting the decorative motifs of the East—China, Persia, India, Turkey, and Arabia—as well as the great styles of the past, from ancient Egypt to the Renaissance. The work was a great success and for many years inspired numerous artists and designers of precious objects.

This new body of knowledge of images from other lands and other times corresponded to the idea of continuous progress (which Baudelaire denounced, prophetically, as an illusion in his review of the 1855 Exposition) in every field: economic, social, and cultural. It was an idea of progress that had arisen out of new techniques and the Industrial Revolution, swift urban development and more modern lifestyles, and spectacular economic growth supported by captains of industry and visionary bankers. In France as well as Belgium, Germany, and Italy, many of these economic players were Saint-Simonians, followers of the doctrine of Claude Henri de Rouvroy, comte de Saint-Simon, dubbed "the first French socialist of the industrial era," who

died in 1825. He criticized the injustice of a society where a minority of idlers exploited a majority of workers, and believed that only an elite of business leaders could put an end to the "landowners and persons of private means," the "leeches of the nation." Specialists and business leaders should govern France. The doctrine of Saint-Simon was little known during his lifetime but gained broad recognition from 1830 onward, thanks to the work of his followers, who originally formed a community to build his churches. Soon Saint-Simonian ideas spread among numerous entrepreneurs, convinced that technical and scientific progress and industrial development should bring about a golden age for all humanity, bosses and workers alike. This was conditional on putting an end to parasitic feudalism and private-income-based capitalism, leaving inventors, engineers, and the enterprising middle class to freely engage in business activities. The considerable economic boom during the Second Empire, and Napoleon III's open-minded attitude toward the movement, would strengthen this new freedom. A number of Saint-Simonians founded the most spectacular business enterprises of the time, such as the brothers Émile and Isaac Péreire, who were major players in the economic modernization of the country: they created the first French railway line, in 1835, between Paris and Saint-Germain, followed by many others; financed a road network; invested in mining spa companies; founded the city of Arcachon; and, above all, established a bank, in 1852—the Société Générale de Crédit Mobilier, designed as a share-holding operation. The establishment of the Crédit Mobilier

was supported by Napoleon III—proclaimed emperor in December—and his family, his half-brother—the duc de Morny—and his government, including his finance minister, Achille Fould. The bank would finance, among other enterprises, the large-scale modernization of Paris directed by Baron Haussmann.

Ferdinand de Lesseps was another illustrious Saint-Simonian, who took up the idea of Prosper Enfantin, one of Saint-Simon's earliest disciples: that of linking the Mediterranean to the Red Sea via a canal in order to facilitate trade between Europe and Asia, and thereby fraternity and prosperity among peoples. Lesseps became a close friend of the Ottoman viceroy of Egypt, Said Pasha, and obtained from him the concession to build the Suez Canal in 1854. After construction work on a colossal scale, the canal was inaugurated in 1869 in the presence of Empress Eugénie.

Napoleon III was in power, but this new middle class of entrepreneurs reigned. Not only on an economic level but also, benefiting involuntarily from a certain indifference on the part of the emperor toward to the arts, on a cultural and artistic level, which it influenced in ways as various as its own diversity.

The decorative arts and architecture were the first areas to be visibly influenced by this technical, economic, and social context, and not only in France. Recent inventions and new forms of labor organization had sometimes spectacular consequences: the Crystal Palace, a huge glass and iron edifice covering 754,000 sq. ft. (74,000 m²), was built in just six months to house London's Great

Exhibition of 1851, using standardized, prefabricated elements—glass panes and iron rods—bolted together floor by floor thanks to new assembly techniques. Electroplating techniques developed in 1837 by the Prussian engineer Moritz von Jacobi began to be used by the Christofle company in 1842, providing the new middle classes with access to inexpensive silverware. In a similar trend toward the "democratization" of fine goods, new processes such as mechanical reduction and molding as well as modern printing techniques led to a host of new decorative items becoming available to this new social class. In Paris, after the opening of the Bon Marché in 1852 by Aristide Boucicaut, which was soon imitated, people could make their purchase at the new *grands magasins* or department stores. In New York, Macy's opened in 1858, while La Rinascente opened in Milan in 1865. In all areas, the division of labor reduced the production costs of crafts that were now organized on an industrial scale: the goldsmith Froment-Meurice and the cabinetmakers Racault Krieger, for example, employed hundreds of skilled workers.

Curiously, aside from these new production methods, industrial rationalization did not lead to any stylistic innovation in the arts. With the orientalists, as mentioned above, the only notable development was an ethnographic concern for realism. While a multitude of machine-made objects might have generated an "art *nouveau*"—a new art—in the West, it was the ancient world and foreign lands that inspired the orientalism, eclecticism, and historicism of the second half of the nineteenth century. Several reasons have been put forward to try to

FACING PAGE AND ABOVE
Jean-Valentin Morel (1794–1860),
WATCH AND CHAIN, 1853–54,
belonging to the duchesse de Luynes,
and its preparatory drawing.
Gold, silver, rubies, bloodstone,
diamonds, fine pearls, and enamel.
Chaumet collection, Paris.

PAGE 162
Henry Dasson (1825–1896),
Louis XVI style gilt and patinated
bronze and amethyst **REVOLVING
DIAL CLOCK**, 1881. The case,
in the form of the Three Graces
wearing diaphanous classical drapery,
supporting a patinated bronze globe
upon a gilded swagged cloth.
The globe set with two rotating chapter
rings with Arabic minute and Roman
numerals painted on enameled
plaques, the time indicated from
above by a gilt arrow held in the hand
of a putto lying alongside a seated
cupid holding his bow. Richard
Redding Antiques, Switzerland.

PAGE 163
JEAN-BAPTISTE CARPEAUX
(1827–1875), *The Four Quarters of the
World Supporting the Celestial Sphere*, 1867.
Musée des Beaux-Arts, Valenciennes.

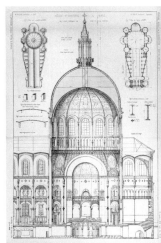

explain this paradox: the absence of an innovative, driving taste that might have been forged by governments; the diversity of a divided middle class; the profusion of compilations of global or historical design motifs, such as Owen Jones's seminal work; the influence of the École des Beaux-Arts, where archaeology and history prevailed; or Romantic principles that prevented a perception of the beauty of forms deriving from a mechanical process. Perhaps, also, in a world undergoing profound social and economic change, there was a need for reassurance provided by references to the past. Never has a period seen such interest in history and archeology, done so much to support museums through gifts of collections of ancient art, or restored so many historical monuments. In a text in 1939 written in French, *Paris, capitale du XIXᵉ siècle*, the German philosopher and aesthetic theorist Walter Benjamin offered another, psychological explanation, suggesting a need to build a private fortress of dreams or escape, to withstand the predominance of utilitarianism and commodity production: "The interior is the asylum of art … The collector dreams his way not only into a distant or bygone world but also into a better one—one in which … things are freed from the drudgery of being useful."[3]

This urge to find refuge in a pre-industrial past was the driving force behind the work of certain decorative artists at the time: in England, William Morris founded the Arts and Crafts movement in 1862, to bring back high-quality, historically inspired craftsmanship; in France, the ceramicist Édouard Avisseau researched the techniques of Bernard Palissy and sought inspiration in Renaissance ceramics; and the painter-enameler Claudius Popelin—for a time the lover of the influential French princess Mathilde Bonaparte, cousin of Napoleon III—revived the "painter's enamel."

So there was nothing "utilitarian" about these dreams of history that appear to have shaped the decorative forms of this period in the throes of a profound transformation. In architecture, eclecticism was the watchword, with Charles Garnier's imposing Paris Opéra, opened in 1875, where baroque was combined with late Renaissance and neoclassicism. On viewing the almost completed monument, the empress is said to have asked the architect if it was in the Louis XV or Louis XIV style, to which Garnier is said to have replied: "It is Napoleon III style!" In the same period, Victor Baltard, built, not far from the Opéra, the church of Saint Augustin, in a masterly blend of baroque and Roman-Byzantine. Architectural eclecticism spread throughout Europe, including Russia—with numerous monuments such as the Grand Kremlin Palace designed by Konstantin Thon—and the United States, with, among others, the many buildings by Richard Morris Hunt, who designed the façade of New York's Metropolitan Museum of Art. Besides eclecticism, architecture also embraced a historicist approach, in favor of one era or another, producing buildings in neo-Roman, neo-Byzantine, neo-Renaissance, neo-Gothic, neo-baroque, and neo-Moorish styles.

In painting, specialists of the historicist, academic or "*pompier*" genre were renowned for their historical or mythological scenes. Two of the most famous of them were the Dutch-born British

FACING PAGE
PIERRE-KARL FABERGÉ (1846–1920),
jeweled egg on plinth, incorporating
a clock and an automaton, 1902.
Gold, silver, enamel, seed pearls and
precious stones. Private collection.

ABOVE
ALFRED STEVENS (1823–1906),
The Bath, c. 1867. The most "Parisian"
of Belgian painters, Stevens produced
numerous interior scenes showing
modern women in intimate settings.
A silver and black pocket watch can be
seen in the background of the picture.
Musée d'Orsay, Paris.

painter Lawrence Alma-Tadema and the Frenchman William Bouguereau. While their work was hugely popular among the general public and certain collectors, their brand of realism, sometimes with sensual overtones, but mostly rather bombastic and cold, met with sharp criticism that would endure for a century. On the occasion of the Salon of 1879, the writer Joris-Karl Huysmans wrote scathingly of Bouguereau: "He has invented gassy paintings, full of air. It's not even porcelain any more; it's flaccid-flawless; it's heaven knows what, something like the limp flesh of a squid."[4]

If Huysmans was so violent in his criticism of this academic painting, it was because he had for several years already been discovering painters who were outlawed, refused, and scandalous but who were the salt of modern painting: after Édouard Manet, who caused a scandal in 1863 with the contemporary female nude in his *Déjeuner sur l'herbe* (*Luncheon on the Grass*, originally *The Bath*), came the Impressionists, whose name derived from the painting first exhibited by Claude Monet in 1874, *Impression, Soleil levant* (*Impression, Sunrise*). It wasn't until the end of the century that the new middle class began to collect them. In the meantime, some of these artists—including Auguste Renoir, Camille Pissarro, Claude Monet, Alfred Sisley, and Berthe Morizot—unable to find a place where they could exhibit their work, created in 1874 the Société Anonyme Coopérative des Artistes Peintres, Sculpteurs et Graveurs, whose first exhibition was that year, in the studio of the photographer Nadar on Boulevard des Capucines, Paris. It was as if the return to intimacy, to sentiment, to *impression*—but this time using light in a decidedly modern manner—was the most natural transition toward the totally new art that would prevail in the twentieth century.

WATCHMAKING
FROM 1850 TO 1895

FACING PAGE
Jean-Eugène Robert-Houdin
(1805–1871), Napoleon III
MYSTERY CLOCK, c. 1860.
The transparent dial shows no
gears and the transmission between
the movement in the pedestal
and the hands remains completely
invisible. Private collection.

———
BELOW
Auguste-Lucien Vérité (1806–1887),
**ASTRONOMICAL CLOCK WITH
AUTOMATA**, c. 1857–60, in the
cathedral of Saint-Jean in Besançon.
Vérité was an engineer and organ
maker from Beauvais. Listed
as a "historic monument" in 1991,
the clock has thirty thousand parts.

The Industrial Revolution brought about as a result of the invention of the steam engine, which was progressively adapted to the locomotive, the ship, and to manufacturing tools, transformed the agricultural and craft economy into an industrial and commercial economy. The fundamental principles of industrial production that were the division of labor, a relative interchangeability of clock components, and the use of steam as a driving force, were implemented in France, Germany, and the United States in the late eighteenth century. A few years later, a uniquely American style emerged, with the "Massachusetts" wall clock, a cross between the European decorative wall clock and the longcase clock, followed by the "banjo" clock in the shape of the musical instrument. The American clock of the second half of the nineteenth century was produced in gigantic factories that sent the European clockmaking industries into an economic slump. In Germany, particularly in the Black Forest, clocks became progressively standardized. Models, decorative features, and prices were determined according to early marketing principles, to be always able to meet the demand of every market. The cuckoo clock, which might today be described as a social phenomenon, combined an industrially produced mechanism with, for the finest models, hand-sculpted decoration by master craftsmen, making them valuable pieces that were both decorative and commercial. In France, the Comtoise clock with its driving weights was industrially produced. It was a popular item and often served as a wedding gift for young couples who would keep it for life. Industrialization divided the production process into two categories: on the one hand, precision mechanisms that were made only by skilled craftsmen, and on the other hand, those manufactured for less expensive but widely sold clocks.

The fashion for pastiche arose in the 1830s and 1840s with the reappearance of the Gothic style, a reaction against the excessive rigor of neoclassicism. A new enthusiasm for the Renaissance preceded a taste for the seventeenth and eighteenth centuries. Furniture, knickknacks, and clocks in styles of the past were produced to varying degrees of quality for all categories of clientele. Identical replicas of certain pieces of royal furniture items were made for the wealthier customers. From 1850, Richard Seymour-Conway, the 4th Marquess of Hertford, natural father of the collector Richard Wallace, played a major role in the market

for highly valuable replicas. He commissioned no fewer than ten reproductions from the most eminent Parisian artists, including the famous Louis XV desk by Jean-Henri Riesener and the astronomical clock with turning sphere by Passemant and Caffieri. For his Herrenchiemsee Castle, Ludwig II of Bavaria had numerous copies made of major clocks at Versailles, including the one by Antoine Morand, and the "Creation of the World" and astronomical clock by Passemant. In the early twentieth century, François Linke, a Parisian cabinetmaker from Bohemia, bought the model of Passemant's astronomical clock in order to make two reproductions of it. In this period, the art of reproduction gained popularity as a showcase of Parisian craftsmanship and also a means of cultural dissemination. Based on the use of traditional techniques, with materials of excellent quality, it was a reaction against industrial progress.

Middle-class families were fond of displaying luxurious and entertaining objects in their living rooms. The market for mechanical paintings had grown to such an extent that the craftsmen who formerly worked on small-scale productions were setting up businesses, filing patents, and sometimes employed several hundred workers. Mechanical paintings in relief with automata were the most popular kind. They served both an aesthetic purpose, in the furnishing of a room, and a utilitarian one, thanks to their small clock. Balloons, steam trains, and sailboats conjured up travel, echoing the technological innovations that were fascinating nineteenth-century society.

The fashion for pastiche led to the rediscovery of the *Recueil d'ouvrages curieux de mathématique et de mécanique* in which Nicolas Grollier de Servière, a seventeenth-century engineer from Lyon, described the mysterious clocks of his invention. Clockmakers were fascinated by his ideas: some reproduced mechanical systems from the past; others built their own mysterious watches and clocks, sometimes in series, filing patents and models. The illusion was perfect when the transmission between the mechanism and the hands mounted on transparent glass disks was totally invisible. And when the dial was linked, via a crescent-moon motif, to a translucent crystal column without any visible gears, the mystery was all the greater. Jean-Eugène Robert-Houdin, clockmaker, illusionist, and electrical pioneer, spearheaded these fascinating objects. Performances of automata, illusions, and conjuring tricks that took place at his theater at the Palais Royal in Paris were popular with high society; it was considered good form to be seen there, and at the opera, in the chic arcades with their luxury boutiques, and at the recently established spa and seaside resorts. The railway and shipping companies enabled people to travel farther and faster. It was in this context that floral clocks made their

appearance. Both ornamental and functional, their decoration changed through the seasons. They were either electric or pneumatic, and formed a connection between nature and technological progress. Industrialization had by now spread to watches, clocks, and turret clocks. In London, the clock installed on one of the towers of the Palace of Westminster was driven by a specially invented gravity escapement. For the cathedrals of Besançon and Beauvais in France, Auguste-Lucien Vérité, clockmaker and civil engineer for the railroad, one of the first to develop the use of electricity in timekeeping, made two astronomical clocks with automata, the first housed in a Renaissance-style dresser, the second, presented at the 1869 Exhibition at the Palais de l'Industrie in Paris, in a piece of furniture in the Roman-Byzantine style.

Now produced using increasingly mechanized processes, watches were either decorated in the traditional manner or adopted a simpler aesthetic. The winding crown, more practical than a key, gradually took over, leading to changes in the shape of the pendant. Fashionable ladies were fond of bejeweled bracelets featuring a removable timepiece that could also be worn on a long necklace. Jewelry ensembles made up of a long necklace, a bracelet, and drop earrings were also popular. A matching watch could be fixed to a necklace or to a brooch, depending on the circumstances. Men's watches, however, were designed to show off their functionality. Physicians, engineers, and military men used chronographs with a plain design, sometimes personalized with a simple monogram. Travelers proudly using the modern means of transportation were more interested in having universal time displayed on their watch than in the decoration of its case. Plain designs were also preferred for the hunter watch, with complication, which had a hinged cover to protect the multi-function dials. The late nineteenth-century men's watch indicated everything that was mechanically measurable and its technicality was an end unto itself. **D.F.**

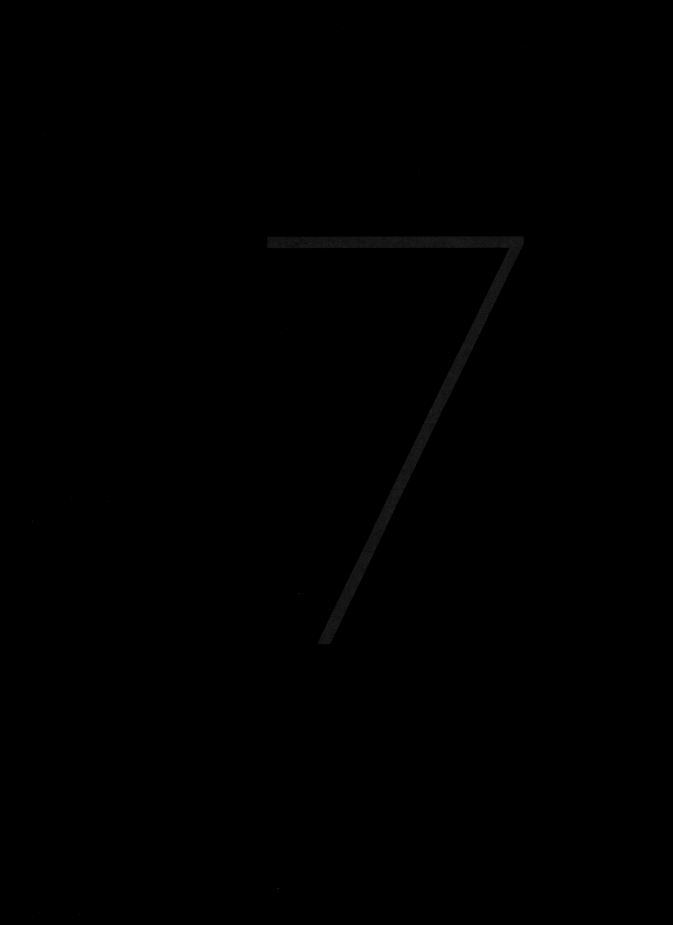

THE TIME OF THE
AVANT-GARDES

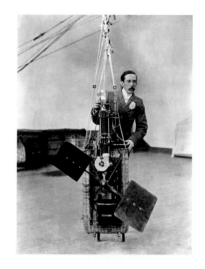

In 1904, Alberto Santos-Dumont, a wealthy thirty-year-old eccentric dandy and heir of a French-born Brazilian "Coffee King," was famous and had been living in Paris for six years. The press never tired of reporting and photographing his exploits in his self-designed flying airships, to the astonishment of Parisian society. His hour of glory came in 1900, when he flew his *Santos-Dumont No. 4*, a cigar-shaped airship over 98 ½ ft. (30 m) long, several times over the Exposition Universelle. The following year, on board the *No. 6*, he took up the extraordinary challenge—and won the 100,000 franc prize—launched by the industrialist Henry Deutsch de la Meurthe: to fly an airship between the Saint-Cloud flying club and the Eiffel Tower and back, a distance of just over 6 ¾ miles (11 km), in under thirty minutes. In 1904, Santos-Dumont, who had long been impressing spectators by his airship flights over Paris, was on his *No. 13*. That year, he asked one of his friends, the jeweler Louis Cartier, to make him a watch with a dial that would be immediately visible while he was at the controls of his airship, and therefore a type of design that was still very rare at the time: a wristwatch. This unique timepiece has since been lost, but in 1908, Cartier designed a square watch, which went on the market just three years later. It is thought to have resembled the 1904 prototype. It was available in gold and in platinum. This model, later named the Santos-Dumont and then the Santos, has been sold to this day.

The Santos has gone down in watchmaking history as the first watch that was designed, down to the smallest detail, to be worn on the wrist in a bracelet (made of leather), thanks to attachments (lugs or horns) that were an integral part of the case, not simply added on to it. But it is also the first known watch whose structure and function directly impacted its aesthetics: the dynamics of its square form, a beveled bezel to enhance the visibility of its functionalities, and exposed nails and screws, foreshadowed an "art moderne" already present in architecture, but that would only appear in watchmaking and jewelry with the true advent of this style in the decorative arts in the 1920s.

The industrial or functional inspiration sweeping Europe and the United States forged the pure lines of art moderne—called "1925 style" or "art deco" after its success at the Exposition Internationale des Arts Décoratifs et Industriels Modernes in Paris in 1925—that became popular in the first years of the century, as a reaction to art nouveau. The latter style had emerged in the early 1890s to break with the repetition of historical styles. But its profuse ornamentation, organic, sometimes mannered forms, and precious symbolism, failed to carry the seeds of any new development and soon brought about its decline.

Early signs of art moderne are visible in the architectural works of the Chicago School; the city saw the construction, after a great fire in 1871, of the first steel-frame buildings allowing non-load-bearing exterior walls and so without any ornamental features to speak of. In 1879, William Le Baron Jenney built the first of them, the First Leiter Building, with seven levels, then in 1885 the Home Insurance Building, which, with its 138 ft. (42 m) in height, ten stories, and 580 windows, was considered the first skyscraper. One of the great

FACING PAGE
Cartier, **SANTOS WRISTWATCH**, Paris, 1916. Platinum, gold, sapphire cabochon, leather strap. Round LeCoultre caliber 126 movement, *fausses Côtes de Genève* decoration, rhodium-plated, eight adjustments, eighteen jewels, Swiss lever escapement, bimetallic balance, Breguet balance spring. Cartier Collection.

ABOVE
ALBERTO SANTOS-DUMONT (1873–1932), a wealthy heir and pioneer of aviation from Brazil, poses elegantly in the basket of his dirigible, *Santos-Dumont n° 1*, c. 1900.

PAGE 182
Napoléon Le Brun (1821–1901), **METROPOLITAN LIFE INSURANCE TOWER**, c. 1910. Both the diameter of the dials of each of the four clocks (26 ft. 3 in./8 m) and the weight of the hands (1100 lbs [500 kg] for the minute hand and 770 lbs [350 kg] for the hour hand) give an idea of the size of the mechanism. New York.

PAGE 183
UMBERTO BOCCIONI (1882–1916), *Unique Forms of Continuity in Space*, 1913. This work by the theoretician of the Futurist movement marks a radical break with art nouveau. Museu de Arte Contemporânea, São Paulo.

masters of the Chicago School, Louis Sullivan, started out at the architectural office of Le Baron Jenney. In turn, he trained a major architect of the modern movement, Frank Lloyd Wright. Influenced by Japanese architecture, which he had seen at the 1893 Chicago World's Fair, Frank Lloyd Wright became, in the early years of the twentieth century, the main representative of the Prairie School, an architectural movement whose aim was to promote harmony between human habitation and the natural environment. Built mostly in the flat expanses of the new residential suburbs, the houses were characterized by their low silhouettes structured by horizontal lines and planes.

A young Austrian student, Adolf Loos, also visited the Chicago Exposition in 1893, and discovered the city's new skyscrapers, then those of New York, where he lived for three years. On his return to Vienna in 1896, he became an architect and theorist of modern architecture, presenting his innovative ideas in a series of articles that brought him fame. In his provocatively titled essay of 1908, *Ornament and Crime*, he denounced excessive ornamentation, in particular that of art nouveau, then caused a scandal with the extremely bare-looking building of reinforced concrete that he built in 1909 on the Michaelerplatz in Vienna, opposite the Hofburg, the imperial palace. In the same period, German architects belonging to the Deutscher Werkbund (German Association of Craftsmen) were also designing industrial-inspired buildings, whose structure determined their design. Exhibited at the 1910 Salon d'Automne in Paris, they found support among a number of French

architects. Among them were Auguste Perret, who built the Théâtre des Champs-Élysées in Paris in reinforced concrete in 1913, and Robert Mallet-Stevens, whose first projects were shown at the Salon d'Automne of 1912 and who would become the most sought-after French architect in the inter-war period. Also in these early years of the 1910s, the German Walter Gropius—who would found the Bauhaus movement in 1920—began his career as an architect inspired by the same principles, while in the Netherlands, geometric abstraction, as illustrated by the painter Piet Mondrian from 1913, would influence, after the war, the interior designers and architects gravitating around the journal *De Stijl* (The Style).

It was after having discovered the cubist works of Braque, Cézanne, and Picasso, in around 1911, that Mondrian began to explore abstraction. Cubism, which emerged in 1906, probably remains the most radical revolution in the history of figurative painting. Not only in proposing a geometric mode of composition that was quite new—Cézanne famously advised his painter friend Émile Bernard to "treat nature by means of the cylinder, the sphere, and the cone"—but more importantly in developing *simultaneity*, or the fragmented depiction of a subject through multiple points of view—a manner adopted by Picasso. Picasso's *Demoiselles d'Avignon*, considered the first cubist work, painted in Paris in 1906–7, was influenced by Cézanne and African art but marked a turning point in the work of Georges Braque and then that of Juan Gris, Francis Picabia, Constantin Brancusi, Robert and

Sonia Delaunay, and Albert Gleizes. Cubism was also experimented with in sculpture—Picasso's, of course, but also that of Alexander Archipenko, Jacques Lipchitz, and Ossip Zadkine.

Fauvism, which appeared in 1905, further contributed to the development of art in the early twentieth century, this time essentially in the field of color. Following in the footsteps of Van Gogh and Gauguin, painters such as Henri Matisse, André Derain, Georges Rouault, Maurice de Vlaminck, Albert Marquet, and Kees Van Dongen had only one obvious point in common: the use of bright, even garish, colors that sometimes were quite unlike the natural tones of the subjects they depicted. This use of color for its own sake would have a considerable influence on art of this period and, later, on abstraction.

Futurism, another artistic movement that emerged in this period, in Italy this time, brought to contemporary art the sweep and shape of its forms. The movement's manifesto, published in 1909 in *Le Figaro*, penned by its founder, Filippo Tommaso Marinetti, proclaimed the beauty of the machine and of speed: "We declare that the splendor of the world has been enriched by a new beauty: the beauty of speed. A racing automobile with its bonnet adorned with great tubes like serpents with explosive breath … is more beautiful than the Victory of Samothrace."[1] The titles of other manifestos, such as *Against Passéist Venice* and *Let's Kill the Moonlight*, also reflected the sometimes violently expressed radicalism of the movement, which sought to put an end to all the forms and sentiments of the past. The titles of some of

the most important art works, dating from 1912 and 1913 and conveying a sense of energy and movement, also spoke for themselves: *Dynamism of the Human Body* and *Dynamism of a Soccer Player* by Umberto Boccioni and *Dynamism of a Dog on a Leash* by Giacomo Balla.

Amid this pre-war artistic proliferation fueling the emergence of a distinctly modern art, two other phenomena played a role: *art nègre*, as traditional African art was called at the time, which became sought after by collectors and whose stylized motifs were borrowed by some artists; and the performances of the Ballets Russes, founded in 1907 by the impresario Serge Diaghilev, whose avant-garde choreography and boldly colorful costumes and sets designed by Léon Bakst stunned audiences avid for new forms.

The years just before World War I saw the first signs of a budding "decorative art," which could only flourish ten years later. For example, the lacquered panels by the France-based Irish artist Eileen Gray, who mixed Japanese-style motifs and geometric abstraction, which she exhibited in 1913 at the Salon des Artistes Décorateurs in Paris. The beginning of the war in 1914 prevented any form of organized artistic activity for several years. On June 28, 1914, the Archduke Franz Ferdinand, heir to the Hapsburg throne, was assassinated in Sarajevo by a Serb nationalist. On July 28, Austria-Hungary declared war on Serbia, and the ensuing alliances dragged much of Europe into the conflict. France and Germany each mobilized a million and a half men, and hostilities began on August 2. For four years, attacks and counter-attacks on every

PAGES 188–189
GIORGIO DE CHIRICO (1888–1978), *Italian Square* (detail), 1914. Known for his metaphysical paintings, the Italian painter introduced references from Antiquity into structured landscapes of apparent simplicity. Private collection.

FACING PAGE
Patek Philippe, **GRANDE COMPLICATION POCKET WATCH**, 1915. Yellow gold case, with perpetual calendar at 6 o'clock, equation of time, phases and age of the moon at 12 o'clock, sunrise and sunset at 9 o'clock and 3 o'clock. Beyer Zurich Clock and Watch Museum.

ABOVE
LÉON BAKST (1866–1924), *Portrait of Sergei Diaghilev with His Grandmother*, 1906. Through the chromatic boldness of his work, the Russian painter and set and costume designer contributed to the birth of modern art. State Russian Museum, Moscow.

ABOVE
Le Corbusier (1887–1965),
photograph of an interior of the
PAVILLON DE L'ESPRIT NOUVEAU.
Presented at the International
Exhibition of Decorative Arts in Paris
in 1925, this innovative building
contrasts with the aesthetic and
architectural conventions of the time.
Musée des Arts décoratifs, Paris.

FACING PAGE
Alfred Dunhill, **WATCH
INCORPORATED INTO A SILVER
BELT BUCKLE**, 1929. A button
opens the buckle and reveals the watch.
In the 1930s, this type of watch
was very much in vogue amongst
sportsmen, especially golfers.

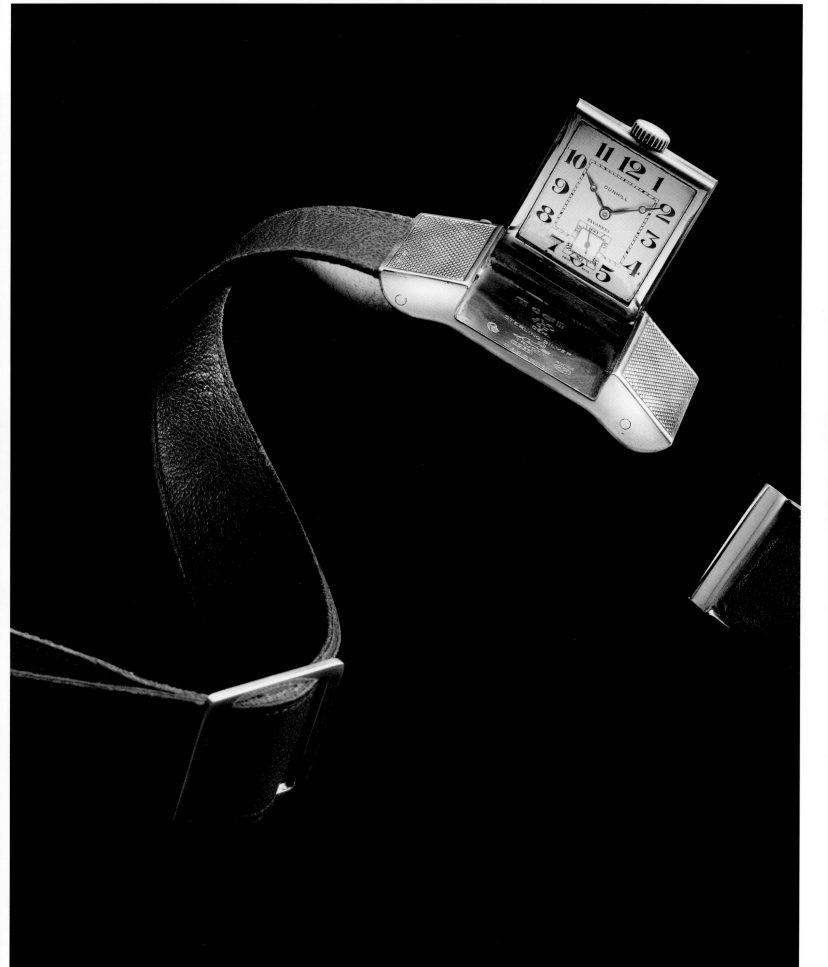

ABOVE

HENRI LEBASQUE (1865–1937), *The Cigarette*, c. 1920. This painting depicts an elegant young woman wearing a watch on her wrist, a habit that became increasingly popular in the 1920s in wealthy circles. La Piscine, Musée d'Art et d'Industrie André Diligent, Roubaix.

FACING PAGE

Audemars Piguet, **WOMAN'S WRISTWATCH WITH JUMPING HOURS**, 1932. This extremely refined design comprises a case of rose gold and white gold. Digital display indicates the hours in a window at 12 o'clock, and minutes in a wider window at 6 o'clock.

PAGE 196

Gilbert Rohde (1894–1944), **ELECTRIC CLOCK**, c. 1933. Between 1932 and 1933, the American designer created a series of clocks, including this one, for the Herman Miller Clock Company, which are remarkable for their avant-garde design. Metropolitan Museum of Art, New York.

PAGE 197

PIET MONDRIAN (1872–1944), *Composition with Blue*, 1926. The master of abstract geometry developed "a new theory for a new world." His work explored the grid and primary colors. Philadelphia Museum of Art, Philadelphia.

front led to a horrifying number of deaths: over thirty-seven million were killed. The writers Louis-Ferdinand Céline in France and Ernst Jünger in Germany would each describe the horror of that absurd war, in their respective masterpieces, *Journey to the End of the Night* and *Storm of Steel*.

The economic, social, and political consequences of the war were also of a scientific and technological order. The conflict boosted progress in aviation, with the development of new engines and more sophisticated measuring and navigational instruments. With the return of peace, these advances brought about the expansion of civil aviation, including postal services as well as freight and passenger transport. For the lucky few, aviation heightened the pleasure of travel, as did the great ocean liners, luxury trains, and the automobile. The war also had moral and psychological consequences that had a deep effect on the Western mentality, as reflected, for example in the advent of the liberated woman, dubbed the "*la garçonne*" in France in a very popular novel by Victor Margueritte in 1922. Women worked in offices and factories, replacing men who had been called up and acquiring a new independence. In France, during the happy decade between the end of the war and the great economical crisis of 1929, called the *Années folles* (literally, the "crazy years," or the Roaring Twenties) many city-dwelling women began to work and discovered a new freedom. They played sport, drove cars, smoked, put on their makeup in public. Couturiers such as Jean Patou, Jeanne Lanvin, Coco Chanel, and Madeleine Vionnet designed silhouettes especially with them in mind: they looked androgynous at first glance but

in fact made women look even more feminine: the corset was dispensed with, slimness was de rigueur, and dresses were straight and knee-length, with a dropped waist. The first women's trousers made their appearance, necklines were low and arms often bared, and hair was cropped short.

This silhouette seemed to echo the geometric and stylized modern decors that were popular in the 1920s. Most of the leading architects and interior designers of the time had started their careers before the war but did not become fully active and famous until after that tragic period, during the Roaring Twenties. Louis Süe and André Mare, who had founded the Atelier Français in 1912, got back together again in 1919 to set up the Compagnie des Arts Français, and were joined by painters, interior designers, and artists such as Paul Vera, Richard Desvallières, Bernard Boutet de Monvel, and André Marty, who produced all sorts of art works, furniture, and decorative objects. The Compagnie was tasked with the Pavillon Fontaine and the Musée d'Art Contemporain at the 1925 Exposition Internationale des Arts Décoratifs et Industriels Modernes.

This event took place in Paris from April to October and featured twenty-one nations—with the notable exceptions of the countries of the two Americas and Germany—as well as all the leading names of the decorative arts. France was naturally well represented, with several pavilions devoted to specific themes, its regions, or the *grands magasins* (department stores). The architect Pierre Patout, who would later design the interiors of three great ocean liners, including the *Normandie*—built the

Porte de la Concorde with its nine great columns, and the Pavillon du Collectionneur, housing an elegant array of objects and furniture items admired by visitors. Many of the exhibits were by the interior and furniture designer Jacques-Émile Ruhlmann, who was in charge of the whole pavilion, and whose taste for traditional French cabinetmaking inspired his own exceptionally refined furniture designs, such as a cylinder desk and a chiffonnier in Macassar ebony and ivory. Furniture and interior designs by Ruhlmann were on display in the pavilion of the French Embassy, where several rooms brilliantly showcased the work of the Société des Artistes Décorateurs: the hall by Robert Mallet-Stevens (who also designed the Pavillon du Tourisme), decorated with works by Fernand Léger and Robert Delaunay; the study-library by Pierre Chareau (today reconstructed at the Musée des Arts Décoratifs in Paris); the dining room by Henri Rapin; and the smoking room by Francis Jourdain. The Pavillon de l'Élégance featured displays by the jeweler Cartier and the couturier Jeanne Lanvin, whose stand was the work of her favorite designer, Armand Rateau. The multidisciplinary artist Jean Dunand, famous for his ornamental brassware, exhibited several monumental vases. He was also, together with the interior designer

Pierre Legrain, one of the great furniture designers of the day; his African-inspired work made use of mahogany, ebony, palm wood, and python skin, among other materials.

In the midst of these pavilions, luxuriously decorated with furniture and objects that showcased fine traditional craftsmanship, stood two buildings like an ode to a more industrial and "democratic" modernity: the very bold pavilion of the Soviet Union by the Constructivist architect Konstantin Melnikov—which would win the exhibition's Grand Prix for Architecture—and the Pavillon de l'Esprit Nouveau, the work of Le Corbusier. The latter illustrated the concepts of "purism" developed in the journal *L'Esprit nouveau* that was founded in 1920 by the Swiss architect with the painter Amédée Ozenfant. Here, apart from a few chairs and tables, there was no furniture or decorative objects, but rather "equipment": not in wood, but in metal, designed to be mass produced, with standard, fitted cupboard spaces built into or attached to the walls in every area of the home where a specific daily function had to be performed. A new avant-garde was born, prefiguring a form of architecture that would, especially after World War II, endeavor to combine low cost and visual appeal. ⧖

WATCHMAKING FROM 1895 TO 1940

FACING PAGE
Jaeger-LeCoultre, **ATMOS CLOCK**,
1936. Thanks to the revolutionary
invention of Jean-Léon Reutter
in 1928, this clock, with its perpetual
movement, rewinds itself automatically,
either as a result of variations in
temperature or atmospheric pressure.

BELOW
Longines, **ROUND POCKET WATCH**,
c.1907. The underside of the silver
case is engraved with a bouquet
of irises. The bezel, the middle, and
the pendant are stamped with art
nouveau motifs.

Following the establishment in 1884 of a Universal Time system and the division of the terrestrial globe into twenty-four time zones, public clocks began to appear everywhere. Progressively, railway stations, government ministries, and hospitals were equipped with networks made up of a master clock and secondary clocks linked to each other by electric cables. The master clock would send out electrical impulses that controlled the display of the time on a series of dials. Paris's brand new Gare de Lyon railway station, built in 1900 so that visitors and foreign delegations could arrive near the site of the Exposition Universelle, was fitted with such a network. Installed in a bell tower that made it the highest clock in the world of its day after London's Big Ben, it featured a mechanism that distributed the time display to the platforms, halls, and waiting rooms. From that time on, new public clocks were also designed to impress and entertain. In Munich, historical and folk scenes with automata were played out in the neo-Gothic bell tower of the city hall. Modeled after the Campanile on Saint Mark's Square in Venice, the Metropolitan Life Insurance Company Tower in New York was both a public clock and a central timekeeper for all of the offices it housed. In the daytime, its bells rang out a Handel melody every fifteen minutes. At night, the chimes were replaced by a red beacon to mark the quarter-hours and a white one for the hours. In the historical center of Vienna, twelve historical figures from the city, alone or in pairs, all in repoussé and polychrome copper, each symbolized an hour. They paraded through a gallery spanning a street between two wings of a building. On the hour, an organ played a melody from the national repertoire. Its design, in the purest Viennese Jugendstil, was the work of Franz von Matsch, a painter to the imperial court. Since the 1920s, the Meissen manufactory has been installing clocks with porcelain bells. Their special sound was popular in many German cities, before spreading to Austria, Finland, Italy, and, in the twenty-first century, Japan.

The global art nouveau movement, which emerged circa 1895, was characterized by its flowing, undulating, sometimes complex lines. Idealized women, flora, and nature all inspired its repertoire. The wristwatch had not yet begun to rival the indoor clock, which was still seen as an important element of interior furnishing. Clocks were decorated with bronze, tin, silver-plated metal, wood, or ceramic, while floor clocks

were made of carved wood with marquetry or moldings. However, the traditionally minded clientele continued to prefer pastiches of designs of the previous centuries.

Art deco emerged in the 1910s as a reaction against the excesses of art nouveau, and became the dominant style of the inter-war period. While quite traditional in its beginnings, the style quickly became more functionalist in spirit, as expressed in clean, spare forms, in a range of materials including wood, bronze, hard stones, marble, mold-pressed glass, enamel, mother-of-pearl, ivory, and shagreen. Following on from the English clocks powered by variations in atmospheric pressure developed by James Cox in the eighteenth century and the Austrian clocks by Friedrich Richter von Lössl in the nineteenth century, the Atmos mechanism in a glass case was developed by Jaeger. Depending on the version, it was driven by variations either in temperature or in atmospheric pressure. Some clocks ran on perpetual motion—seemingly powered by the spirit of the times.

In the 1920s, precious materials were used to produce clocks of various shapes and sizes, combining the arts of jewelry and clockmaking. They were designed by prestigious names such as Boucheron, Mauboussin, Van Cleef & Arpels, and, especially, Cartier. Designs by Cartier often incorporated statuettes and carved hard stones from the eighteenth and nineteenth centuries, as well as animals from the jeweler's bestiary, including carps and tortoises. Inspired by the works of Jean-Eugène Robert-Houdin, Cartier presented in 1912 its first mystery clock in a rock crystal case called Model A. It was made exclusively for the jeweler by the clockmaker Maurice Coüet. The two gear trains of the plates supporting the hands were replaced by a single-train system. Three years later, the driving mechanism was housed in the upper part of the "portique"-type models. These two innovations considerably broadened the scope for creative design.

On its timid appearance circa 1875, the wristwatch was, unlike the pocket watch, described as a mere adornment, a costume watch. It had to find its own identity and personality, and rid itself of its historic constraints before it could forge a reputation as a respectable timepiece. Originally round in shape, watch cases became oval, rectangular, or square. Cut-off corners led to the octagon, to the combination of rectangle and oval, and to the barrel. While the mechanism's basic form determined the shape of the watch case—the movement's protective cocoon—jewelers could be creative in defining and imposing their own styles and influencing the lines (as with Cartier's integrated lugs), forms, and decoration. After World War I, cases took on clean, geometric shapes,

a trend highlighted at the 1925 Exposition Internationale des Arts décoratifs in Paris. The fabulous palette of colors offered by stones tempered the rigor and purity of the form. Following the monochromatic hues of the late 1910s, jewelry pieces became black and white, with the combination of diamond and onyx popular in the early 1920s; colors began to be added in 1925. The baguette shape, with a mechanism built on two levels, and aperture watches would dominate the decade of the 1930s. All these designs remained in line with the art deco style, as illustrated by the Jaeger-LeCoultre Reverso watch, among others. **D.F.**

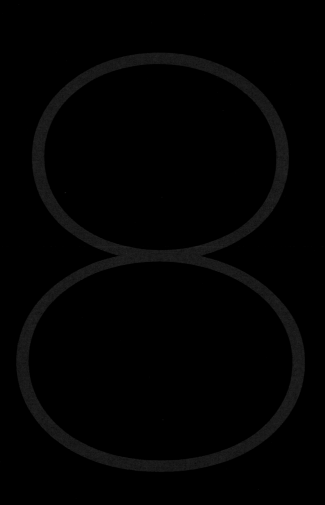

TIME
FOR ALL

In the year 2000, the London collector James Dowling donated thirteen watches from different periods to the British Museum. Today, only two of them, Swiss-made quartz wristwatches, are on display in the museum's Room 39 devoted to clocks and watches: an Omega Marine Chronometer, which, on its release in 1974, was the first quartz watch of its kind, adopted by numerous yachtsmen including Éric Tabarly and Jacques Cousteau; and a very economical Swatch Wipeout (a surfing term for a fall off the board) brought out in 1989. While the former is exhibited partly for its innovative features, the latter is presented more as a work of art, with its contrasting orange and black and multiple motifs in the bright and bold surfer style. It is a perfect specimen of industrial design, representative of an era in which inexpensive, everyday objects enjoyed a sophisticated level of design. Launched in 1983 by the entrepreneur Nicolas Hayek, Swatch watches were reasonably priced (due to the fact that they were mass-produced with a simple mechanism), accurate thanks to their quartz movement, and had a particularly creative design. Certain models were the work of famous artists, including Keith Haring, Kiki Picasso, Valerio Adami, Pol Bury, Pierre Alechinsky, Vivienne Westwood, and Christian Lacroix. Swatch became one of the symbolic objects of a phenomenon that emerged after World War II: the combination, in different ways, of art with everyday consumer objects.

History's most tragic event, World War II with its sixty million victims, shook up the very idea of humanity: man's intelligence could serve a cold, reasoned cruelty missing from the animal kingdom, and used in a meticulously organized form of savagery. In addition to the death and destruction, and the catastrophe of Europe in ruins, the horror of this unforeseen inhumanity cast a dark shadow. Immediately after the war, the judgments of the Nuremberg trials—which established the definition of "crimes against humanity" for the first time—and the creation of the United Nations— whose charter determines to "reaffirm faith in fundamental human rights, in the dignity and worth of the human person"—were the first institutional responses to this universal and more or less conscious sense of anxiety. Others responses would come from the intellectual elite, with, for example, the concepts of freedom and responsibility offered by Sartrean existentialism. But the postwar period brought new fears: that of nuclear weapons, and that of the Cold War, an increasingly virulent antagonism between the Communist bloc and the Western nations dominated by the United States.

The best response to these uncertainties would eventually come from the West's extraordinary optimism in the face of newfound peace and freedom and the vast reconstruction effort. With jazz, Hollywood cinema, blue jeans, and sodas, Europe enjoyed a taste of the modern "American way of life." The Marshall Plan helped to achieve rapid reconstruction, generating powerful economic development to the benefit of all. Then came the advent of "consumer society," as defined for the first time by the French Marxist sociologist Henri Lefebvre in the 1950s, and reflected in the annual Salon des Arts Ménagers (Household Arts Show).

FACING PAGE
Omega, **MEGAQUARTZ 2400 MARINE CHRONOMETER**, 1974. With its analogical dial, this watch preserves the aesthetic features of a traditional watch despite being fitted with a quartz movement, and borrows from the design of a tonneau watch. Given the use of steel for the case and the type of strap, it conformed with the growing trend for sports-chic watches. British Museum, London.

—

ABOVE
The French yachtsman **ÉRIC TABARLY** in 1976, training for the Transat solo regatta aboard his trimaran, *Pen Duick VI*. On his wrist, he wears an Omega Marine Chronometer.

—

PAGE 210
ROBERT RAUSCHENBERG (1925–2008), *Untitled* 1979. The artist is considered one of the precursors of pop art. He was instrumental in devising the "Combine", in which everyday objects were incorporated into the painting.

—

PAGE 211
Similar to an eye wide open to the world, this astonishing arrivals and departures board (1958) is the work of the American architect of Finnish origin **EERO SAARINEN** (1910–1961). TWA Flight Center at Idlewild Airport, now John F. Kennedy International Airport, New York.

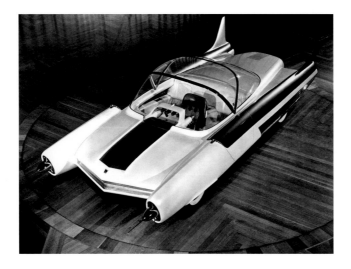

ABOVE
The aerodynamic and futuristic look of the **FORD FX ATMOS**, a revolutionary concept car designed in 1953 by American industrial designer Richard Arbib (1917–1995). In the 1950s, the automotive industry was the sector of choice for many designers.

FACING PAGE
Hamilton Electric, **VENTURA WRISTWATCH**, Lancaster PA (USA), 1957. The first mechanical wristwatch with traditional balance to be powered by an electric battery. In yellow gold, the asymmetrical triangular case of a resolutely avant-garde style was designed by Richard Arbib. Beyer Zurich Clock and Watch Museum.

PAGES 214–215
ROMAN OPALKA (1931–2011), *Details 1965/1 - ∞*. Beginning in 1965, and fascinated by the passage of time, the painter began counting from 1 to infinity on his canvases, which thus reveal a subtly poetic sequence of uninterrupted figures.

Postwar artists responded in different ways to this frenetic consumption of objects and goods, which seemed to have become the be-all and end-all in developed industrial societies: they produced consumer objects themselves; they depicted the object in its industrial dimension; or they made spontaneous, ephemeral work that became a kind of consumer good in its own right. Whatever the case, the aim of these artists was to produce art that represented the new economic reality, in such a manner that demanded the adhesion and even participation of the consumer public. And in every case, it was also about making art and beauty accessible to the greatest number, in different ways.

The first of these approaches was illustrated in the considerable development of industrial design, pioneered by a Frenchman who had settled in the United States at a young age: Raymond Loewy. The father of "streamline," which he defined as "beauty through function and simplification," Loewy was the brilliant inventor of the design for the Studebaker car, Lucky Strike cigarettes, and the company logos of BP, Shell, Exxon, and LU cookies. Later, in the 1960s and 1970s, he also designed the interior of the supersonic aircraft Concorde, and that of the Skylab space station. In 1956, the Finnish-born American architect and designer Eero Saarinen came up with his Tulip Chair, which was produced by the furniture manufacturer Knoll and became famous worldwide. Other great designers of the time include the Milanese architect Gio Ponti, a master of Italian design since he had founded the magazine *Domus* in 1928. Besides major architectural works—for

example the Pirelli Building in Milan in the late 1950s and the Denver Art Museum ten years later—Ponti created a number of successful designs for companies, such as his La Cornuta espresso machine for bars with its very "industrial" look, produced by La Pavoni. His household designs included tableware and his range of sanitary ware for the American company Ideal Standard in 1954.

The depiction of the industrial object and its trappings in painting and sculpture was another way of bringing the new economic reality into art. Pop art, born in England in the 1950s and rapidly adopted in the United States, used mass-produced everyday items and images from advertising, television, and comic strips, with little or no modification, often with an element of humor. The collage of the London artist Richard Hamilton, *Just what is it that makes today's homes so different, so appealing?*, which was used as the poster for the exhibition *This Is Tomorrow* at the Whitechapel Gallery in London in 1956, is often considered the inaugural work of pop art: it was made up of fragments of advertisements cut out of American magazines, arranged in an imaginary interior. An equivalent movement emerged in France, nouveau réalisme, represented by a range of very different artists, some of whose work fully embraced the spirit of pop art, such as that of Arman with his *Accumulations* of consumer objects, César with his compressed cars, and Martial Raysse with his assemblages or arrangements of everyday plastic objects. Pop art reached its peak in the United States in the 1950s and 1960s. Robert Rauschenberg mixed painting

ANDY WARHOL (1928–1987), *Untitled*, c. 1950. In the New York of the 1950s, the appropriately named "Pope of pop" was already a talented publicist. Prolific and offbeat, he revealed an innate gift for drawing associated with unlimited creativity. Private collection.

FACING PAGE
JASPER JOHNS (b. 1930), *Untitled*, 1986–87. This artist lies between abstract expressionism and pop art. Like his friend Rauschenberg, Johns takes a real object (in this case a watch), which he replicates in painting. Private collection.

PAGE 218
ROY LICHTENSTEIN (1923–1997), *Still Life with Clock and Roses,*1975. In the 1960s, the American painter incorporated popular imagery and comic strips in his work, using techniques used in printing.

PAGE 219
Lip, **MACH 2000**, 1975. This watch by Roger Tallon retains the usual functions (analogue display, a traditional caliber, adjustment of time using the crown, strap with a pin buckle), but the design nevertheless does away with the concept of the jewel-watch by sweeping aside the shackles of classic watchmaking forms.

and sculpture in his "Combines," incorporating used objects that looked as if they'd been salvaged from a dump; James Rosenquist used the billboard technique to create large-scale images of a dish drainer, for example, or tubes of lipstick; while Roy Lichtenstein borrowed images from comic strips. From 1962 on, Andy Warhol, the most famous pop artist of all, painted banknotes, food cans and other packaging from major food brands (Campbell, Kellogg's, Heinz), and bottles of Coca-Cola. Yet it was more his technique—silk-screen printing on canvas enabling him to reproduce a motif as many times as he wished, a technique he also used for his portraits of celebrities—that made his work the symbol of an art that reflected the mass-production economy.

The third way used by artists as a means to illustrate the proliferation of consumer objects was the most radical: the work itself, ephemeral by nature, was offered up for consumption. "Offered up" being the appropriate term, because this approach was often a criticism of art as merchandise. In the field of "urban" or street art, the pictorial form of expression, created by artists who sometimes worked anonymously, was a modern version of an ancient technique: graffiti. In New York in the 1970s, there appeared paintings produced illegally, on walls and subway cars, which were not works to be sold but images destined to disappear. Two artists with very different styles, friends of Andy Warhol, who would both soon become famous after switching to a different genre, were the leading representatives of this New York graffiti art: Jean-Michel Basquiat

and Keith Haring. Graffiti and tagging soon spread all over the world, leading to the emergence of a number of stars with highly recognizable styles of their own, such as, in France, Ernest Pignon-Ernest and Jef Aérosol.

Another art form challenging the longevity and marketable status of the artwork, an ephemeral artistic event called a "happening," performance, or installation, played a key role in those years. The first known happening promoted as such was organized in 1952 by a musician and visual artist influenced by the dada movement and Marcel Duchamp: John Cage, at Black Mountain College, an experimental college founded in 1933 in North Carolina that was attended by many of America's avant-garde artists. The 1952 event featured a canvas by Robert Rauschenberg, a ballet by Merce Cunningham, a poem by Charles Olsen recited by the author perched on a ladder, and a piece of music by David Tudor. Three years later in Japan, the Gutai group founded by Jiro Yoshihara, which included artists such as Murakami Saburo, Shiraga Kazuo, and Tetsumi Kudo, began its happenings before an audience that was invited to participate, tearing paper screens, painting with their feet or body rolled in mud, and then destroying the canvas, using fire, throwing inflatable balloons, and so on. In the 1960s, this type of artistic practice frequently took place in the United States and then in Europe, after the first performance in 1959 by a student of John Cage's, Allan Kaprow, at the Reuben Gallery in New York: *18 Happenings in Six Parts*. He asked the spectators to change place—chairs were arranged randomly—between each

performance of the work, mixing music, dance, the appearance of panels, and other actions that, as the artist explained, "meant nothing." Among the first happening artists, also inspired by John Cage, was the Lithuanian-born American George Maciunas, founder in the early 1960s of the Fluxus movement, some of whose members would go on to become celebrities, including the German Joseph Beuys, the Japanese Yoko Ono, the Korean Nam June Paik, and the Frenchman Ben.

In 1963, an installation by Nam June Paik at the Galerie Parnass in Wuppertal, Germany, comprising thirteen television sets with images distorted by the interference of a sound frequency in their cathode ray tube, marked the beginnings of "video art." It was initially an artistic take on that mass medium, television broadcasting, brought to American and European homes via what was by now a cult object. With technological progress and the advent of portable cameras, video gradually became a means to create images, as illustrated by the founder of the genre and by artists such as the Americans Bruce Nauman and Dan Graham, or the Frenchman Fred Forest. Technology, electronics, and electricity were now all part of this dematerialization of the artwork, with artists who created "light art," for example, a movement born just after World War II and that developed through the 1960s. "Instead of a brush, we use light," said the Italian artist Bruno Munari in 1954, recalling Picasso's light drawings of 1949, traced in the air in a darkened studio with a simple handheld light and captured by the photographer Gjon Mili. Artists used light to create captivating experiences that

plunged the viewer into magical luminous environments, using fluorescent tubes or other light sources. Among the most famous of them during this period were Dan Flavin, Martial Raysse, James Turrell, and François Morellet.

Two other approaches, even more spectacular but more marginal, challenged the traditional status of the work of art in a radical way. "Body art," stemming from the ideas of John Cage and his various followers, emerged in Vienna in the 1960s with a group formed by the artists Hermann Nitsch, Otto Muehl, and Günter Brus. It used the human body in blasphemous "actions" that were often considered scandalous. In 1965, at the Galerie Schmela in Düsseldorf, Joseph Beuys coated his face with honey and gold powder and spoke about painting to a dead hare. The artist subjected his or her body to all sorts of experiences, sometimes painful ordeals—such as the self-inflicted wounds by the Frenchwoman Gina Pane—turning it into a language that often served to convey radical social criticism. Another approach, "land art," very different in its spatial dimension but also a means of protest, arose, again in the 1960s, out of the idea of site-specificity in art, seeking to remove it from its elitist confinement to an interior, gallery, or museum. It sometimes conveyed an ecological concern, such as *Time Landscape* by Alan Sonfist, in 1965, which was the re-creation, over some 1,000 sq. ft. (100 m²) and on the site itself, of the native forest as it would have appeared on Manhattan Island before the arrival of the European colonizers. Other artists were more interested in nature in its existing

state as a basis for the work. Some, most of them American, gained recognition in 1968 with the exhibition *Earthworks* at the Dwan Gallery in New York: Carl Andre, Robert Smithson, Dennis Oppenheim, Robert Morris, and Herbert Bayer, among others.

The various artistic experiments of the 1950s through to the 1970s, some of which would continue into the following decades (urban art, ephemeral installations, land art) were thus rooted in a desire to question the status of the work of art as a marketable object, a questioning that was itself part of a more global political movement: criticism of a capitalist, materialist, and consumerist system. This movement gathered momentum among students and led, from the mid 1960s, to the birth of two currents of protest. The first was a revolutionary movement that manifested itself in Europe, during a period of political violence lasting until the 1980s, in the emergence of political terrorist groups that carried out attacks and kidnappings. The other adopted the opposite approach—the hippie movement, which was non-violent and laid-back, hedonistic and pacifist in spirit, was born in the United States in the wake of the literary movement of the Beat Generation, embodied by the writers William Burroughs, Allen Ginsberg, and Jack Kerouac. Characterized by the use of recreational drugs, communal living, "free love," a taste for "psychedelic" music, and closeness to nature, the movement also manifested itself in styles of clothing and graphic art that broke with bourgeois middle-class conventions and featured bright colors, exuberant forms inspired by the use of drugs, and "unisex" floral patterns. But soon, the economic downturn sparked by the oil crisis in the 1970s, and, especially, the neoliberalism of the following century—which also saw the collapse of the Communist bloc and the advent of the Internet—would bring back a taste for individualism and social success, and put an end to utopian visions. The work of art, once more seen as an object of consumption, and sometimes of speculative investment, often regained its traditional status, amid a plethora of new museums and private collections, and popular exhibitions. ⌛

WATCHMAKING FROM 1950 TO 2000

From the 1950s onward, as central heating replaced the use of fireplaces, the decorative clock almost completely disappeared from home interiors. Wristwatches took over, as they were now reliable, and the time gradually came to be displayed on household appliances and, later, on computers. Small desk and bedside clocks were still popular, but these were functional, mass-produced items that were little more than a dial in a featureless case. Only jewelers and a few of the historic specialist houses produced designs that were also works of art.

The monumental clock has always been a standard-bearer of public timekeeping. Because of its appeal in places drawing large numbers of visitors, architects often incorporated clocks in their projects. An astronomical clock was installed in the main concourse of Paris's Orly Airport; it works in real time, while the movements of the Earth and the Moon are speeded up to catch the eye of travelers. The steam clock in Vancouver was a tribute to the engineer James Watt. A mini engine running on steam provided by the city's heating system raises the clock's driving weights and operates a whistle chime that plays the Westminster Quarters. Near the Centre Georges Pompidou in Paris, a monumental electronic clock operated a battle between a man and a bird, a dragon, or a crab—symbols of the sky, the earth, and the sea, respectively. Three times a day, these creatures, made by Jacques Monestier, launched a frontal attack on their adversary, to the sound of crashing ocean waves and storms. In Frankfurt, a gigantic Swatch watch measuring 530 ft. (162 m) long was hung down the side of the Commerzbank Tower, part artistic installation, part marketing ploy.

Another monumental work of public art, and a nod to the history of the railways, was a clock installed at the Cergy-Saint Christophe train station, northwest of Paris. In 1985 it was named the largest in Europe. The Time-Flow Clock, created by the physicist and artist Bernard Gitton, appeared in different versions around the world. It operates based on an ancient system using water, known as a clepsydra (water clock) and a pendulum. Hours and minutes are accurately displayed with a shimmering colored liquid in a maze of transparent spheres and tubes.

Other public clocks included calculators accurate to 1/300,000th of a second, designed for the countdown of the number of seconds left to the year 2000. The one in Paris, named Le Génitron, was showing more than 400 million seconds on its inauguration in 1987.

Quality wristwatches of the early 1950s had either an automatic or hand-wound mechanism protected by an anti-shock system and housed in a waterproof case made of so-called unbreakable glass. At the end of World War II, the miniaturization of movements prompted the growth of particularly elegant ultra-thin cases. Their spare, clean look was accentuated from the mid 1950s by dials with numerals and indices marked simply by lines.

At a time when scientists and sportsmen were impressing audiences with their exploits, Blancpain's Fifty Fathoms watch was popularized by the ocean explorer Jacques Cousteau, who wore it on his wrist during the shoot of *The Silent World*. This cult documentary film revealed the wonders and colors of the ocean depths. Eterna's KonTiki model was a tribute to the Norwegian adventurer Thor Heyerdahl and his raft crossing from Peru to Polynesia. The ascent of the long-unconquered great Himalayan and Alpine peaks and the Antarctic expeditions gave young people a taste for wearing sports watches with altimeter and barometer. The Monaco chronograph by Heuer, precursor of the oversized watches, became iconic when Steve McQueen wore it in the film *Le Mans*.

With the miniaturization of batteries, the watches of the early 1950s could at last be a part of the history of electric clockmaking that had begun over a hundred years previously. First of all, electrical energy replaced mechanical energy to power the traditional escapement. As a mirror of an optimistic era, such an avant-garde object could only be given a futuristic design. In the United States, Hamilton commissioned Richard Arbib, a renowned designer in the automobile industry. He borrowed the V-shaped grille of the Hudson, a car produced by the American Motors Corporation. Turning it 90 degrees, he created an asymmetrical shape that became the hallmark of the Ventura, the first electrical, battery-powered watch in the world, as well as the Pacer and the Meteor, all by Hamilton. No sooner was it invented than electromechanics looked to electronics to use a tuning fork as a regulator. The result was a watch, made famous by Bulova under the name Accutron, with a completely open dial that revealed the mechanism's parts. In 1965, the accuracy of such timepieces equaled that of traditional chronometers, but by the end of the decade, quartz had exceeded the best scores of mechanical and tuning-fork movements.

Very soon, watch thicknesses started to diminish, shrinking from the $7/64$ in. (3.10 mm) of the Piaget's Caliber 7P in 1976 to the $5/64$ in. (2.9 mm) of the ultra-thin Seiko the following year. Records were broken one after the other, with knock-on effects on the size and decor of watches. Thus, the cases of the Delirium I to IV of Longines, Concord, Eterna and Omega,

FACING PAGE
Bulova, **ELECTRONIC ACCUTRON WRISTWATCH**, 1960. With
its stainless-steel case without a dial,
this became the first model
to be fitted with a tuning fork
as regulating organ. Beyer Zurich
Clock and Watch Museum.

the movements for which are supplied by ESA/ETA and have a respective height of 1.98 mm, 1.48 mm, and 0.98 mm ($^5/_{64}$, $^1/_{16}$ and $^1/_{32}$ in.).

New technology and miniaturization ushered in unimaginable new developments: numerical display using light-emitting diodes and later liquid crystals, sometimes in combination; multifunctional watches, dictionaries, calculators, and television. LED and liquid crystal display gave rise to digital art, rooted in the pop art movement. Multi-functional watches, with their industrial-design look, would be abandoned by watchmakers with the revival of the traditional timepiece.

In the face of the devastating effects of quartz on mechanical watchmaking, a resistance movement undertook to reinvent the classic watch. During the second half of the twentieth century, prestigious watchmaking firms began to approach non-specialist designers. Patek Philippe partnered with Gilbert Albert, Heuer with Richard Sapper, Junghans with Max Bill, and Lip with Michel Boyer, Jean Dinh Van, Marc Held, Rudolf Meyer, and Roger Tallon. Nonetheless, given the complexity of the watch, by the late 1960s and early 1970s a new generation of specialist designers had emerged, the most notable of which was Gérald Genta. There was also a new, well-off, dynamic, and sporty clientele. Watchmakers set out to meet their demands, with the Royal Oak by Audemars Piguet, the Nautilus by Patek Philippe, and the Bulgari-Bulgari by Bulgari, among others. Steel took on the aura of a precious metal, while Piaget's Polo line stayed with white gold. Chopard's Happy Diamonds intrigued with its weightless-looking diamonds. These prominently sized, iconic timepieces are among the precursors of today's designs.

Unfortunately, such feats of design were not enough to revitalize a watchmaking industry inundated with electronic components massively produced in Japan. In the absence of large production quantities, there was no hope that its revival could be achieved through a regeneration of its core activity. Switzerland therefore decided to tackle Japanese watchmaking on its own ground. The Swatch, a clever mixture of design, quality, and Swiss tradition, using innovative technology, electronics, and plastic, was launched at a highly competitive price in the United States and then in Europe. It was a global phenomenon, because of its look and myriad colors and designs, and it relaunched the Swiss watch, whose true renaissance in fact lay in high-end, rare, and precious timepieces.

The return to the traditional watch owes much to the lack of emotion generated by quartz watches, to their technology devoid of artistic appeal, and to their mysteriously programmed complications. But the

BELOW
PIAGET WRISTWATCH,1976.
White gold, lapis-lazuli dial, Piaget
7P ultra-thin quartz movement.
Piaget private collection.

FACING PAGE
In 1976, an original expression of
horological creativity revolutionized
the watchmaking world.
Chopard's first **HAPPY DIAMONDS**
model was a men's watch with an
onyx base. The Happy Diamonds
concept consists of a dial topped by
two sapphire crystal plates with
free-spinning diamonds between them.

association of high-tech watchmaking and precious watchmaking would give rise to a new world. A new generation of talented young designers demonstrated the complementarity between handmade and series-produced timepieces. The craftsmanship that had been forgotten since the arrival of electronics had to be patiently relearned and revived before the minute repeater, perpetual calendar, tourbillon, split-seconds chronograph, astrolabe, and planisphere could be accommodated in cases that had become quite a bit larger in size. On the occasion of Patek Philippe's one hundred and fiftieth anniversary, the Caliber 89 symbolized the renaissance of watchmaking for the Geneva manufactory's master watchmakers, and for those of the profession as a whole. **D.F.**

TIME
AND BEYOND

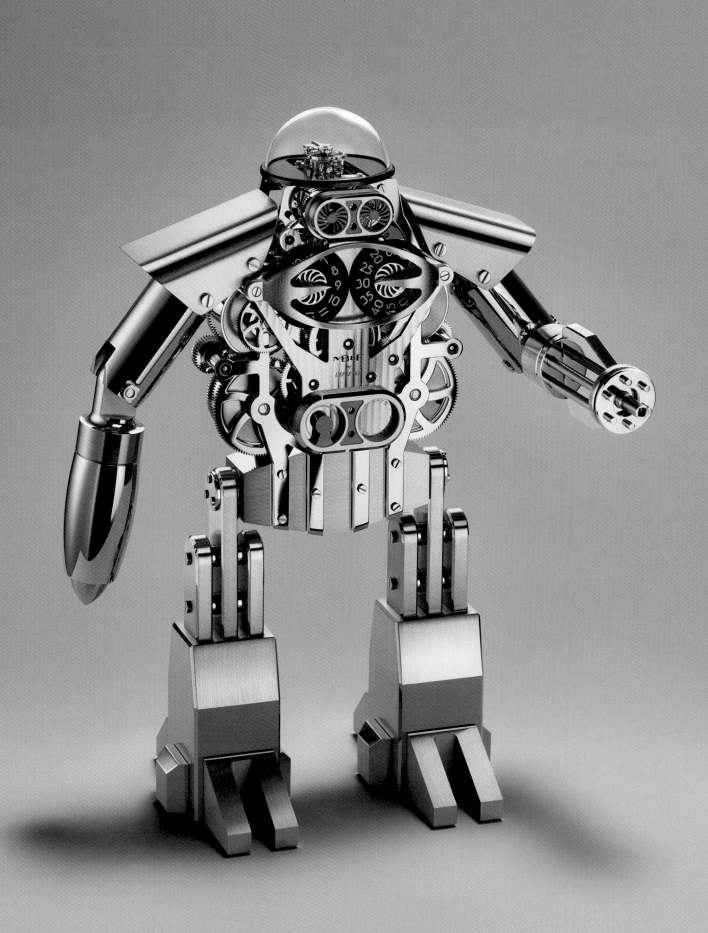

The twenty-first century truly began on September 11, 2001, at 14 hours, 2 minutes, and 59 seconds Universal Time. At that precise moment, in a beautiful blue sky, a United Airlines Boeing 767 flew into the South Tower of the World Trade Center in New York City. The event was watched live throughout the world by millions of viewers already glued to the TV, because for the last quarter of an hour it had been broadcasting images of what people still believed to be an accident: thick smoke was billowing out of the North Tower that had also been hit by a plane. The second explosion left no doubt that this was a terrorist attack, and one that would soon prove to be the deadliest on US soil in history. The events of 9/11 and the almost three thousand victims they caused changed the world. A sense of danger spread through every continent, ushering in draconian security measures. Other attacks, less spectacular but sometimes causing many victims, would follow, one after the other, targeting the populations of numerous countries. Thus has the twenty-first century been the first period in history in which civilians are being affected on a daily basis, throughout the globe, by a hitherto marginal phenomenon: terrorism.

The consequences of this new state of affairs have naturally been many and various. The underlying anxiety that it generates has brought about a certain vigilance and mistrust, a tendency to withdraw into oneself or into the family circle. People are naturally more apprehensive about long-distance travel, preferring destinations closer to home. There has been a return to what

seems familiar and safe, to aesthetics that feel reassuring. In the field of design, big brands have been delving into their heritage for inspiration, bringing in more harmonious, elegant, and ever-classic lines from their past. In 2003, for example, the car manufacturer Jaguar brought out a new model with lines inspired by one launched in 1968. The trend is perceptible in almost all everyday devices and machines, in particular cars and household appliances. Numerous clockmakers also looked to their history for new designs that borrowed from the magnificent aesthetic features of watches from the distant or not so distance past, but were equipped with cutting-edge mechanisms. A recent and exceptional example is Vacheron-Constantin's Référence 57260, released in 2015 for the Genevan firm's two hundred and sixtieth anniversary: a splendid pocket watch similar to those that were still worn in the early twentieth century, but powered by a mechanism with fifty-seven extremely high-tech complications—an absolute record.

On a more fundamental level, 9/11 also changed the relationship between image and history. For the first time, a mass crime came across as a kind of show, designed by the terrorists like a performance, and one watched by millions of people—a show whose undeniable power to transfix lies in our fascination with the image of death and the obscure sentiments and sense of aversion it arouses. Is that comparable to the fascination generated by certain works of art? Less than a week after the tragedy, the composer Karlheinz Stockhausen put his finger on the question and scandalized people by

FACING PAGE
MB&F with L'Épée 1839, **ROBOCLOCK MELCHIOR**, 2015. Jumping hours and sweeping minutes on Melchior's chest are displayed via discs; a dial on its abdomen is the power reserve (forty days) indicator. The retrograde action of Melchior's eyes marks off intervals of twenty seconds. Visible manually wound movement. Limited edition of ninety-nine pieces.

——

PAGES 240–241
PIERRE HUYGHE, *I Do Not Own Modern Times*, 2006. Born in 1962, this multi-talented French artist offers a tense dialectic between reality and fiction, revealed through an intangible relationship to time.

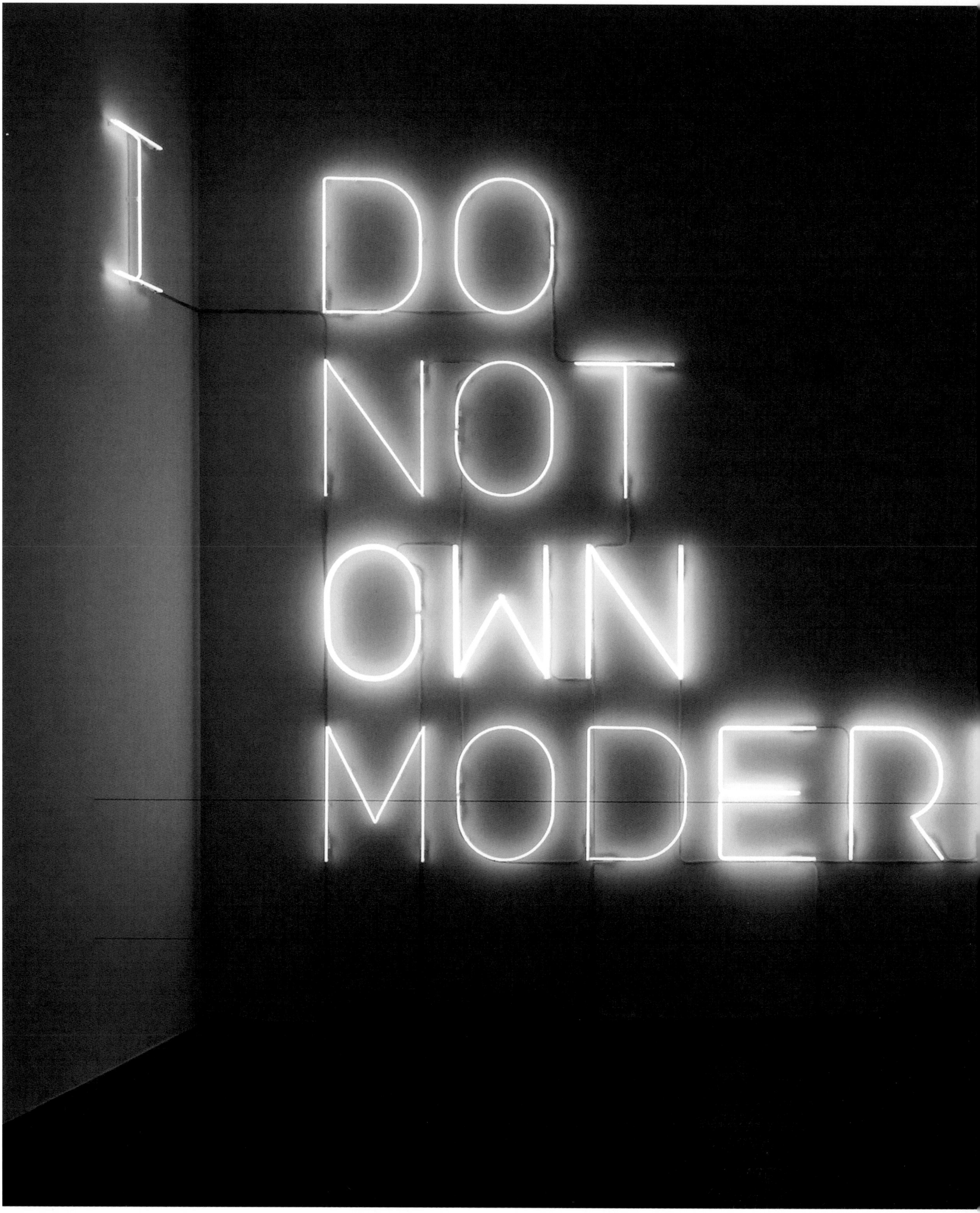
I
DO
NOT
OWN
MODER

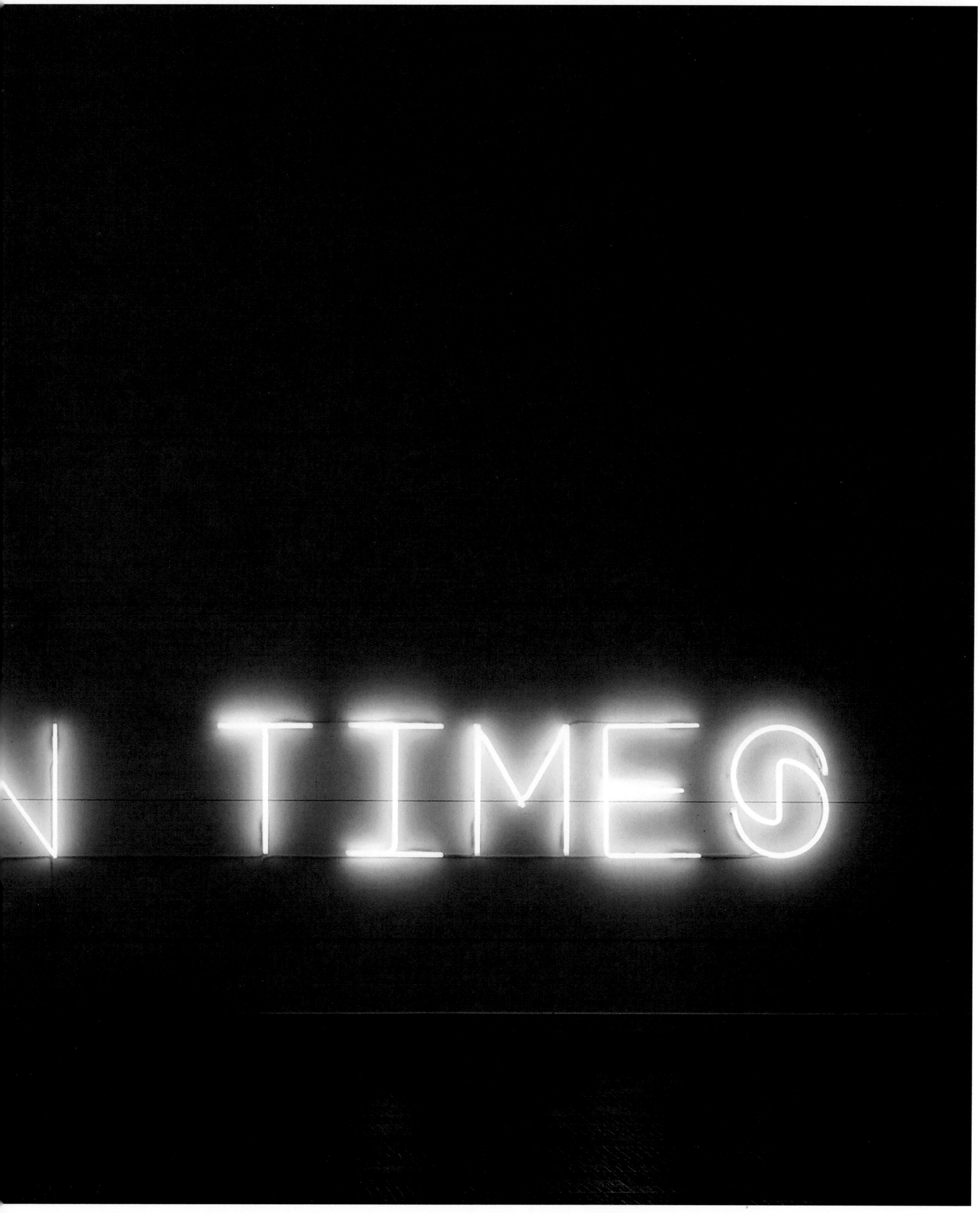
N TIMES

declaring that it was "the greatest work of art that exists." Perhaps that is the reason why few artists have used its haunting images. There is perhaps, also, a certain caution with regard to the notion of "history painting." And the feeling, as expressed by the French artist Stéphane Pencréac'h in 2015, that to depict the event, designed by its authors as a show, "is in a certain way to replay it and therefore to perpetuate the terrorist act."

The German painter Gerhard Richter was one of the first artists of our time, and one of the greatest—he is today considered the highest-selling living painter in the world—to depict the tragedy on canvas. Born in Dresden in 1932, Richter trained in East Germany before crossing to the West in 1961, where he discovered and explored contemporary abstract art and pop art. However, it was the practice of photography that led him to the figurative pictorial style that would bring him fame, with the use of black and white and blurred images. In 1988, he painted *October 18, 1977*, a series of fifteen paintings, based on photographs, of the Baader-Meinhof Gang, a far-left German terrorist organization, which now hangs in MoMA, New York. The painter has said that he hopes that these paintings will, "by way of reporting … contribute to an appreciation of [our time], to see it as it is."[1] The same approach led him, in 2005, to compose an oil on canvas on the theme of September 11, titled *September*. Struck through with horizontal lines, the two towers, clouded in thick smoke but against a background of blue sky, appear to be under the effect of a blast: that of the planes that have penetrated them, and that of the viewer's own stupefaction.

At around the same time, three well-known artists were working on ways to depict or put into perspective the founding event of the twenty-first century. In 2003, the Moroccan artist Mounir Fatmi—who commented "we have all inherited the post 9/11 world"—began his project *Save Manhattan*. A shadow of a composition of books (including two copies of the Koran, representing the twin towers) and a pile of VHS cassettes is projected onto the wall, with ninety loudspeakers emitting the sounds of the urban hubbub, recreating the Manhattan skyline before the destruction of the towers. Fatmi's third installation, *Save Manhattan 03*, was exhibited at the 2007 Venice Biennale. The two other artists of repute that portrayed the event in this period drew their material from the Internet. The German photographer Thomas Ruff—who has experimented with large-format printing and spearheaded, with Andreas Gursky, the Düsseldorf School of photographers who studied at the city's Arts Academy—has been working since the 1990s with digital images, photos, and films selected from the Internet. His *Jpegs* series, completed in 2007, are blow-ups of these digital photographs, to a format of around 8 ft. 2 in. × 5 ft. (2.5 × 1.5 m), in order to bring out their pixelization, in other words, the structure, imperceptible to the naked eye, of the computer-generated images of our daily life. Among them is one of Manhattan filled with the smoke of the twin towers.

The Catalan artist and photographer Joan Fontcuberta adopted an equally striking approach, even more closely related to the Internet. In his

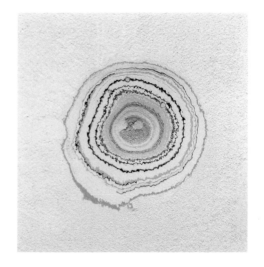

series *Googlegrams*, executed between 2003 and 2007, the artist recomposed powerful images using free photo mosaic software. Each photo was reconstructed like a mosaic made up of eight to ten thousand images found with the search engine Google, using certain key words. His *Googlegram 04: 11-S NY*, dating from 2005, a diptych showing the September 11 attacks, was made up of images found after keying in the words Allah and Yahweh in Spanish, French, and English.

More recently, in 2010, the South African-born Dutch artist Marlene Dumas, whose spare, expressionist works explore intense themes such as death, sexuality, and violence, created *Osama*, a portrait of Osama bin Laden, leader of Al-Qaeda and mastermind of the September 11 attacks. The gentle, smiling expression of the terrorist responsible for them caused a scandal—as if Evil, to be what it is, must not present an engaging appearance. This provocative canvas was acquired in 2012 by the Stedelijk Museum in Amsterdam.

The Internet itself is another major societal phenomenon of our time. In 2017, the number of users was nearly four billion, in other words half of the world's population. Almost three billion of them were registered on social networks. By enabling communication in every form, providing instant access to information, knowledge, buying, and consumption of all kinds of goods, this new tool, permanently accessible to all, has turned lifestyles upside down. Connected devices that can be carried around, most commonly the mobile phone, demonstrate its most advanced technological usages. The first telephones connected to the

Internet appeared in the 1990s, with new models released over the years in step with technological advances in network access. With nearly one and a half billion units sold every year, smartphones are, today, and by far, the most popular technological instrument in the world. The first smartwatch appeared in the early 2010s, but, despite intense promotion and development of its design—as with the Apple Watch launched in 2015—it has not managed to conquer a public that is already over-equipped with technological devices. These "watches" that aren't really watches, because showing the time is not their principle purpose, will probably go down in watchmaking history as a passing phase.

For certain artists, the World Wide Web has become an indispensable artistic medium. As the Chinese artist Ai Weiwei declared to a French magazine in 2012, when he was experiencing harassment from the authorities in his country: "I am not allowed to leave Beijing and I can no longer travel overseas. Frankly, I'm not too badly off. If I'd been prevented from accessing the Internet and Twitter, that would have been much harder." The son of a poet named an "enemy of the people" under the Cultural Revolution, Ai Weiwei had a childhood in difficult conditions, which determined both his artistic vocation and his political activism. In 1981, at the age of twenty-four, he managed to leave China and settled in New York. He produced paintings, photography, and a style of sculpture inspired by Marcel Duchamp's "ready-mades." When he returned to China in 1993, he created many provocative works, installations, and

FACING PAGE
Jaquet Droz, **CHARMING BIRD**. 18-karat white gold case. Sapphire dial. Singing bird automaton movement with hand-wound mechanical movement and push-button automaton triggering mechanism. Sapphire whistle system. Hours-minutes self-winding mechanical movement. Power reserve of thirty-eight hours. Limited edition of twenty-eight pieces.

ABOVE
PIERRE HUYGHE (b. 1965), *Timekeeper*, 1999. This French artist likes to strip off and sand the walls of the various galleries in which he exhibits. By revealing the different layers of paint, Huyghe establishes a surprising parallel between past and future.

PAGES 248–249
Parmigiani Fleurier, **HIPPOLOGIA CLOCK**, 2016. Featuring two thousand two hundred components. Eight-day power reserve. Its base houses two mechanisms side by side, one connected to the automaton, the other to the time display. The window set with white and champagne diamonds shows the hours and minutes over three hours, as well as the scale which can be used to adjust the operation of the automata to the desired time. The mare and her foal are designed as a clock movement. The head, tail, and hooves are cast in silver and hand-polished by a jeweler. Their bodies feature a hand-engraved decoration.

FACING PAGE
Bovet 1822, **RÉCITAL 18 SHOOTING
STAR®**, 2016. Double patents.
Five-day tourbillon, hemispheric
universal worldwide time with
selectable time zone and ultra-compact
twenty-four cities indicator,
hemispheric precision moon phase,
jumping hours, retrograde minutes.
Limited edition of fifty pieces.

PAGES 252–253
CHIHARU SHIOTA (b.1972), *In Silence*,
2008. The work of this Japanese
artist is distinguished by the use of
black woven threads that transforms
beings and objects as though caught
in a gigantic spider's web.

events, placing the Coca-Cola logo on authentic Han or Tang dynasty vases, for example, and organizing an exhibition of controversial photographs titled *Fuck Off* in Shanghai in 2000. Four years later, he founded his own architecture studio, Fake Design, and contributed to the design of the Beijing Olympic stadium, nicknamed the Bird's Nest, by the Swiss architecture firm Herzog & de Meuron. In 2005, on the request of the Chinese Internet portal Sina, he started a blog that immediately became his principle remote channel of political expression and artistic creation. His installation *Fairy Tale*—shown at the Documenta 12 contemporary art exhibition in Kassel, Germany, in 2007, which consisted in inviting 1001 Chinese people from every walk of life to visit Kassel dressed in a "tourist uniform" of the artist's design—was entirely conceived via his blog. Ai Weiwei did it again two years later with the installation *Remembering*. He managed to bring together in Munich nine thousand colored backpacks placed against a wall, arranged to form a phrase in Chinese that had been uttered some time earlier by a mother who had lost her child, one of the thousands of schoolchildren who died as a result of the 2008 Sichuan earthquake: "She lived happily for seven years in this world."

Numerous Asian artists have now made a name for themselves on the art market, producing original and powerful works that have been exhibited in the greatest public institutions. Two of them are the Chinese painter and sculptor Yue Minjun, whose large-scale exhibition at the Fondation Cartier pour l'Art Contemporain in Paris in 2012–13, *L'Ombre du Fou-Rire*, introduced visitors to his unclassifiable work, revolving around brilliant variations of his laughing self-portrait; and the Japanese artist Chiharu Shiota, whose installations often feature tangled wool thread, metal rods, or cables, evoking gigantic spiderwebs, in which the objects of our past, whether close or distant, clear or blurred, are imprisoned yet unchanged over time, just as in our memory.

Intellectuals and artists use the Internet—and all prominent figures now have their own websites—as an indispensable information and promotional tool. While nothing can replace the direct contemplation of a work of art, through the sole authenticity of a gaze laid directly on its material presence, never has art been so accessible, visible, and shareable. In 2004, Google, the biggest player in the sector, launched its Google Books service: the localization and digitization of millions of books in libraries, in order to render them accessible to all via a search engine, either online or by indicating the places where they are kept. The enterprise was challenged, and certain authors and publishers took legal action, but in most cases agreements were reached. Google Books is today the largest textual corpus in the world. In 2011, the company repeated the initiative, this time in the field of the arts, launching its Google Art Project service, renamed Google Arts & Culture. To date, tens of thousands of art works in more than twelve hundred leading museums and archival centers have been digitized, uploaded, and made accessible via a search engine. Thanks to the quality of the digitization, each work can be

examined closely, over the whole of its surface, which is often impossible in situ. Sometimes a virtual tour of the museum is possible.

Digital technology has thus enabled a good half of the world's population to have access, at any time, and free of charge, to major works by great contemporary artists. The most famous of them are present in this gigantic virtual museum, often exhibiting some of their most recent works. Among them is the controversial artist Jeff Koons, creator of kitsch works inspired by pop art. In 2008 the Château de Versailles opened its seventeenth-century rooms to his giant aluminum *Lobster* and his inflatable *Rabbit* in stainless steel, while a sculpture made of one hundred thousand flowers forming the head of creature half-horse, half-dinosaur was exhibited in the gardens of the Orangerie. The Google "museum" currently exhibits four works by this artist, currently one of the most sought-after in the world, including one of his inflatables—a yellow flower from 2012 that belongs to the Ullens Center for Contemporary Art in Beijing.

Another major artist whose work can now be explored on a computer screen or mobile device is the Englishman Damien Hirst. He became famous in 1993, when he was not yet thirty, with his exhibit at the Venice Biennale, *Mother and Child (Divided)*: a cow and calf bisected and preserved in formaldehyde solution in four glass tanks. The artist pursued this provocative animal theme for several years—angering animal rights groups—moving from formaldehyde to other substances with his series of fly paintings with real,

dead butterflies or flies stuck in paint. In 2007, Hirst caused a sensation by selling his work *For the Love of God*, a platinum cast of an eighteenth-century human skull encrusted with 8,601 diamonds, for a sum close to one hundred million dollars.

Several very different works by the great British artist Anish Kapoor are also exhibited in Google's virtual museum. Kapoor produces mostly sculpture, sometimes inspired by images from his native India and often on a monumental scale, with strong, single colors, polished surfaces, shadowy reliefs, passages into which visitors can penetrate, and a sound environment, designed to arouse unfamiliar sensations and an intense emotion in the viewer. In 2011, he dedicated a majestic sculpture inflated with helium, *Leviathan*, to Ai Weiwei. It was displayed at the biennial exhibition Monumenta at the Grand Palais in Paris. Visitors could enter the huge structure—occupying 2,542,656 cubic ft. (72,000 m³) and soaring to a height of 115 ft. (35 m)—and immerse themselves in a red-colored space like an immense refuge, a mother's womb in which the artist offered "a contemplative and poetic experience."

The principle of Monumenta is to invite a contemporary artist to appropriate the vast glass and steel space of the Grand Palais with a new work. The first guest artist, in 2007, was the great German artist Anselm Kiefer, several of whose major works dating from 1969 to 2011 can be viewed on Google Arts & Culture. Kiefer's work is steeped in cultural, mythological, and historical references—those of his native country, as well as, since the 1990s, the Kabala. Often monumental, mixing painting and

FACING PAGE AND ABOVE
Greubel Forsey, **ART PIECE 1**. This audacious co-creation contains within it a work of art in the form of a micro sculpture (facing page), visible only through a unique optical system. The display of time becomes secondary and the open architecture of the timepiece integrates the Double Tourbillon 30°, the first invention by Robert Greubel and Stephen Forsey.

PAGES 256–275
Swedish collective **HUMANS SINCE 1982**, *A Million Times*, 2013. Measuring 13 ft. 1 in. × 6 ft. 6 in. (4 × 2 m), this kinetic sculpture covered with 288 clocks synchronized by iPad was designed by Per Eman and Bastian Bischoff in partnership with Australian engineer David Cox.

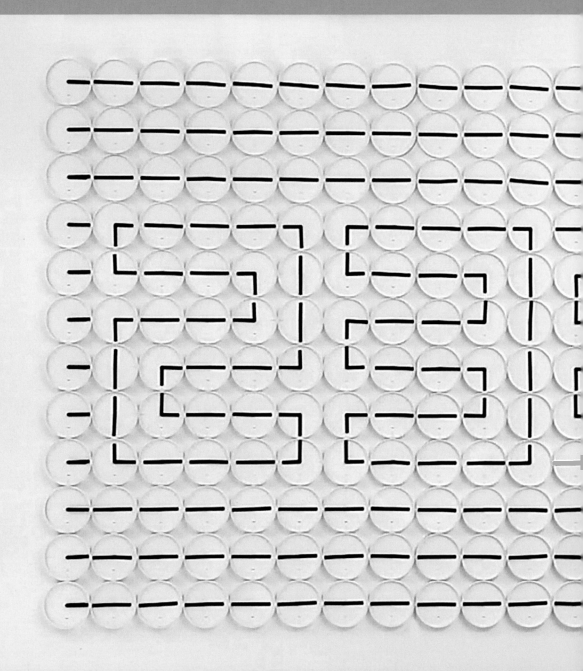

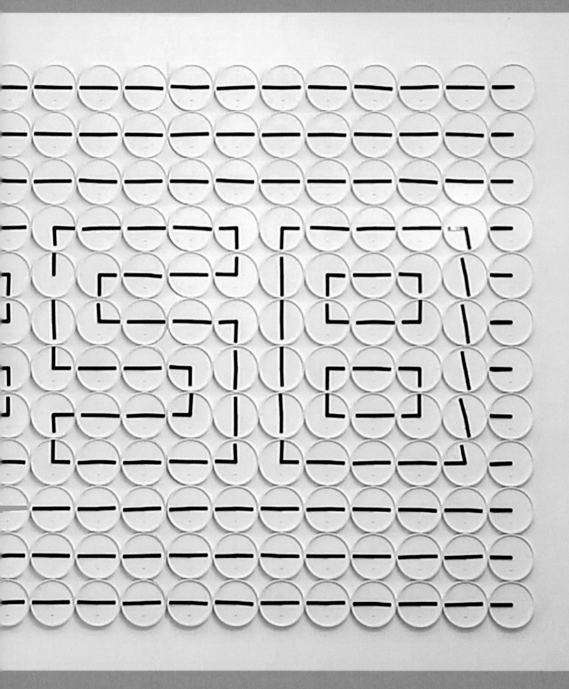

ABOVE
JAN FABRE (b.1958), *Adsum Qui Feci
(I, Here Before You, Am the Guilty Party)*,
2016. Through his often controversial
work, this Belgian artist presents
a provocative and offbeat world view.

FACING PAGE
Richard Mille, **RM 19-02 TOURBILLON
FLEUR**, 2015. The mainplate
skeletonized and engraved by hand.
Mechanism with automaton at
7 o'clock. Resembling the flower
of the magnolia, the petals open every
five minutes and reveal the flying
tourbillon which, when the petals
open, rises slightly to emphasize
all its components. Limited edition
of thirty pieces.

sculpture, they echo a collective human memory haunted by disasters and grief, but also by the magic of its cosmology. The work he exhibited at the Grand Palais was *Falling Stars*, a group of monumental works installed in seven vast "houses," dedicated to German-language poets associated with remembrance, and closely connected in their lifetime: the Romanian-born Paul Celan and the Austrian Ingeborg Bachmann. Featuring ancient Egyptian and Aztec motifs, the Milky Way, a variation on Céline's *Journey to the End of the Night*, rows of books made of lead looking on the verge of collapse, a reference to Palm Sunday … so many themes inviting the visitor to inhabit places of memory from a universal past, by losing themselves within them and then finding themselves.

While contemporary artists often express the violence and absurdity of contemporary societies in a sort of confusion verging on the grotesque, and although they all benefit from the extraordinary universal exposure provided by the Internet, they have not, perhaps for the first time in history, formed particular schools or trends or styles that might mark an era. What could there possibly be in common between the Scottish artist Peter Doig, some of whose painted work resembles a dizzying pastiche of art's historic styles; the Spaniard Miquel Barceló, inspired by African and cave painting; the Belgian Jan Fabre and his deliberately shocking and sometimes cruel performances; the Frenchman Pierre Huyghe, whose protean and highly conceptual work questions our relationship with image and fiction; and—to end a list that could be much, much longer—the Italian sculptor Maurizio Cattelan, with his corrosive humor, whose most famous works depict a pint-sized Adolf Hitler kneeling and praying (*Him*), Pope John Paul II struck down by a meteorite (*La Nona Ora* or *The Ninth Hour*), and a 36 ft. (11 m) marble middle-finger gesture installed in front of the Italian stock exchange in Milan (*L.O.V.E.*)? What do they have in common? Nothing, apparently. Or else, perhaps, that unseemly finger given to the ills of the contemporary world, as a sort of cry to express their faith in art, their hope for humankind, and their freedom. ⌛

WATCHMAKING TODAY

FACING PAGE

MAKKAH ROYAL CLOCK TOWER, Mecca, 2016. The largest clock in the world today dominates the Great Mosque at a height of over 1,970 ft. (600 m). Measuring about 130 ft. (40 m) in diameter, the four dials of the clock are visible from a distance of more than 7 ½ miles (12 km) by day and over 10 miles (17 km) by night, thanks to a lighting system installed on the faces.

———

BELOW

Beat Haldimann, **H9 REDUCTION.** Devoid of both dial and hands, with this wristwatch sight gives way to hearing. Only the sound of the clockwork movement beneath a smoked glass enables the wearer to gauge the passage of time, tick-tock after tick-tock.

The transition from 1999 to 2000 brought with it two concerns relating to timekeeping. One was a fear that a fault in the design and programming of the date change in computing equipment would cause serious malfunctioning in data processing. The second was a curious debate, now long since settled, on the determination of the first year of the millennium, or century, owing to the absence of a year zero. The milestone passed without mishap, however, and the measurement of time, as materialized by clocks and watches, continues to govern our lives.

To call worshipers to prayer, a clock that is today the largest in the world was installed at the top of the 1,970 ft. (600 m) Makkah Royal Clock Tower in Mecca. It is mechanically driven but controlled by cesium atomic clocks, and measures six times larger than those of Westminster. Like a beacon, its illuminated dials spanning 130 ft. (40 m) in diameter are visible for miles around. New automata, as lifelike in appearance as their predecessors, emanate a kind of poetry, propitious for reflection. Since 2007, the climber in Jacques Monestier's monumental work *Le Grand Escaladeur* ascends a crack in a rock face and shows the months, days, hours, minutes, and seconds as he passes by the indices on his way up. In the world of androids, the automaton *Charlie*, commissioned by Jaquet Droz and made to resemble the actor Johnny Depp in his role as Willy Wonka, lifts bells to reveal wristwatches by the firm.

In the early 2000s, the high-tech watch and the precious watch brought together two complementary worlds, in which the designer turned to technology and the jeweler became a watchmaker. The notion of fine, technical watchmaking (what is known as *haute horlogerie* in French) was quick to develop, thanks to the larger size of timepieces, among other factors. This broadened the means of expressing technical as well as aesthetic beauty. The widely touted use of materials borrowed from cutting-edge industries improved the lightness, hardness, and resistance of casings or did away with the need to lubricate certain mechanisms. Endless new models with multiple and beautifully presented complications were launched. However, they soon led to costly studies of energy optimization. Complex escapements developed over a long period of time enabled the display of fractions such as 1/20th, 1/100th, or even 1/1000th of a second. However spectacular, such pieces developed as concepts and produced on a very small scale could only be acquired by a tiny number of watch enthusiasts.

A new trend emerged in 2007–8, a rebellion against the tendency to live life too fast. It sought to produce a powerful emotional charge that would spark a reflection on the philosophy of time. The H8 Flying Sculptura by Beat Haldimann did not display the time as such; it is suggested only by the movement of its tourbillon. It was followed by the H9: without dial or hands, its deep black crystal concealed a tourbillon whose ticking accompanied the passing of time. Hublot adopted a playful approach in its Key of Time, which enabled the wearer to "modulate" the speed of time by accelerating or slowing down the watch on demand. After its Grandes Heures model, with a small hand that moved at a variable speed, Hermès brought out Le Temps Suspendu, in which all the temporary indications could be suspended and the date made to disappear. In Harry Winston's Opus 11, every sixty minutes the numeral of the past hour disintegrated and then reformed as the numeral of the new hour. These unconventional works, highly intellectual in both their design and the curiosity they aroused, gave way to pieces that showcased the craftsmanship of watchmaking, a trend launched notably by Vacheron Constantin in the early 2000s. Crafts from the past that had all but disappeared were revived, and many used again for the first time in watchmaking. Cartier used agate cameo work and minute grains of gold as in the ancient Etruscan granulation technique. Piaget made use of gold thread embroidery on silk and tiny glass tesserae. Vacheron Constantin combined several enameling techniques. Van Cleef & Arpels employed carved mother-of-pearl, plique-à-jour enamel (a cloisonné technique using unbacked, translucent enamel) and cabochonné enamel (creating a relief effect). Grand Seiko brought back piqué, which is mother-of-pearl encrusted with gold and platinum filigree. Harry Winston dials featured marquetry of painted feathers, and those of Chanel and Hermès fine embroidery and the millefiori glass technique, respectively. Other designers made use of minuscule tesserae to form mosaics and wood or straw marquetry.

Automata started to appear in wristwatches. Jaquet Droz created nesting birds, a nod to the work of its founder in the eighteenth century. Bulgari staged a commedia dell'arte scene. Ulysse Nardin stayed with bell-ringers, with its Hannibal Jaquemarts Minute Repeater, or introduced an element of eroticism with the Sonnerie en Passant Erotica and the Hourstriker Pin-up.

In 2015, the launch of the Apple Watch smartwatch sent tremors through the luxury watchmaking business. Responding to the expectations of a young clientele permanently connected to the Internet, it was not the first of its kind, but the power of its inventor was a cause for concern. After this wake-up call, traditional watch design shifted toward

FACING PAGE
Hermès, **ARCEAU TIME SUSPENDED**, 2011. The watch is equipped with a triple retrograde display: 360° retrograde hour and minute hand, retrograde date hand. Function for starting and stopping the hands (making time stand still) by pressing a pushbutton. Self-winding mechanical movement.

———

BELOW
Ulysse Nardin, **HANNIBAL MINUTES REPEATER**, 2015. The figures of the dial—Hannibal and his warriors, transformed into bellstrikers—are, like the landscape and the mountains in the background, carved in 18-karat white gold and mounted on a granite background. The minute repeater is animated by a caliber with one-minute tourbillon visible through the dial. Limited edition of thirty pieces.

a discreet classicism. Since the early 2000s, the continued success of more affordable, neo-retro watches suggested a certain nostalgia for less oppressive times. Vintage models provided a sense of reassurance and reflected a loss of interest in the extravagant watches of the recent past. Ostentatiousness was replaced by a taste for quiet beauty and luxury for one's own enjoyment. Low-key designs and a drastic reduction in size marked a return to the fundamentals of watchmaking and, especially, to watches that were easy to wear and, paradoxically, easier to read.

But each to their own dream: for some, a watch for oneself; for others, an extraordinary technical timepiece; for others still, a work of poetry.

Vacheron Constantin took up the concept of timekeepers with very high complications initiated by Abraham-Louis Breguet. In 2015 it presented its Référence 57260, a piece with fifty-seven complications, "the most complicated watch ever made." The complications included Hebrew and Gregorian perpetual calendars, an astronomical calendar, Westminster chimes, an armillary sphere tourbillon, and a double retrograde split-seconds chronograph. It was a work of traditional craftsmanship and yet highly futuristic, as reflected in the dozen or so patents filed for its design.

In another, equally spectacular register, the Fée Ondine Automaton presented by Van Cleef & Arpels in 2017 is a bejeweled tableau of a fairy sitting on a water-lily leaf. The leaf undulates as a flower opens, releasing a butterfly. Meanwhile, a ladybug marks the hour as it slowly advances. According to its designers, this extremely delicate automaton will serve as an inspiration for future designs.

Thanks to an initiative by the Foundation of the Grand Prix d'Horlogerie de Genève, time measurement was defined, in 2012, as the "twelfth art." Whatever definition you choose to give art, the word derives from the Latin *ars* or *artem*, which means skill, craft, craftsmanship, or technical knowledge, which, curiously, are the bases of clock- and watchmaking. Although observers have often conceded that modern and contemporary arts have abandoned the notion of timelessness as well as that highly subjective one of beauty, to the extent that no particular style has marked the present century, it is an undeniable fact that the art of measuring time has, from its beginnings, been nourished by works of the past, ceaselessly reinterpreted, and tirelessly enriched. **D.F.**

FACING PAGE AND ABOVE
Van Cleef & Arpels, **FÉE ONDINE
AUTOMATON EXTRAORDINARY
OBJECT**, 2017. Engraved and
enameled silver strips, white gold,
rose gold, diamonds, pink sapphires.
Fairy in white gold, diamonds,
sapphires, milky aquamarine, plique-
à-jour enamel. Water lilies in silver,
enamel, yellow gold, diamonds,
yellow and orange sapphires. Butterfly
in white gold, diamonds, pink
sapphires, Australian white opal.
Ladybird in pink gold, white gold,
diamonds, rubies in Traditional
Mystery Set™. Automaton with
animation on demand; five cycles of
fifty-second animation are available
when the mechanism is fully wound.
Manual-winding mechanical
movement, retrograde hour, eight-day
power reserve. Unique piece.

NOTES

FACING PAGE
ALAINPERS, *60 minutes Opalescentes*. Lumino-kinetic creation with 72 pieces of blown glass lighting up progressively.

THE TIME OF THE CATHEDRALS
1. C.F.C. Beeson, *English Church Clocks, 1280-1850* (London: Antiquarian Horological Society, 1971), p. 16, quoted by David S. Landes, *Revolution in Time* (Cambridge, Mass. and London: The Belknap Press of Harvard University Press, 1983), p. 77.
2. Trans. Mary Whittall (University of Cambridge Press, 2010).
3. *Le Livre des faits et bonnes mœurs du roi Charles V le Sage* (1404) [*The Book of the Deeds and Good Character of King Charles V, the Wise*], trans. Judith Laird, unpublished PhD thesis (University of Colorado at Boulder, 1987).
4. "The season has shed its mantle / Of wind, cold, and rain. / And has clothed itself in an embroidery / Of sun gleaming bright and fair."
5. *Decameron (The First Day)*, trans. Cormac Ó Cuilleanáin, based on John Payne's 1886 translation (Wordsworth, 2004).

THE TIME OF THE GRAND SIÈCLE
1. Letter to Chantelou of April 7, 1642.
2. Letter to Chamblay of March 1, 1665.
3. David. S. Landes, *Revolution in Time: Clocks and the Making of the Modern World* (Cambridge, Mass. and London: The Belknap Press of Harvard University Press, 1983), p. 128.

THE TIME OF THE ENLIGHTENMENT
1. An Answer to the Question: "What is Enlightenment?" Quoted in *Kant: Political Writings*, ed. H.S. Reiss (Cambridge University Press, 1991), p. 54.
2. *Histoires de peintures* (Paris: Éditions Denoël, 2004).
3. Quoted in Melissa Hyde, *Making Up the Rococo: François Boucher and His Critics* (Getty Publications, 2006), p. 3.
4. Daniel Roche, *The Culture of Clothing: Dress and Fashion in the Ancien Régime*, trans. Jean Birrell (Cambridge University Press, 1996).

THE TIME OF MODERNITY
1. Farid Chenoune, *A History of Men's Fashion*, trans. Deke Dusinberre (Paris: Flammarion, 1993), p. 21.
2. "The Universal Exhibition of 1855," *Baudelaire: Selected Writings on Art and Artists*, trans. P.E. Charvet (Cambridge University Press, 1981), p. 132.
3. "Eugène Delacroix, Letters and Notes from His Voyage to North Africa." Retrieved from www.csus.edu (California State University, Sacramento).

THE TIME OF INDUSTRY AND ENTERPRISE
1. *Baudelaire: Selected Writings on Art and Artists*, trans. P.E. Charvet (Cambridge University Press, 1981), p. 115.
2. Ibid., p 116.
3. "Paris, the Capital of the Nineteenth Century," in *Walter Benjamin. Selected Writings: 1935–1938*, (Princeton: Harvard University Press, 2002).
4. In *Écrits sur l'art* (Paris: Flammarion, 2008).

THE TIME OF THE AVANT-GARDES
1. Quoted in *After the Future*, Franco Berardi (Oakland: AK Press, 2011), p. 21.

TIME AND BEYOND
1. Quoted in "Gerhard Richter. *October 18, 1977*, 1988," gallery label from "*Out of Time: A Contemporary View*," August 30, 2006–April 9, 2007. Text retrieved from https://www.moma.org/collection/works/79037

APPENDIXES

SELECTED BIBLIOGRAPHY

THE TIME OF THE CATHEDRALS

Barbieri, Roberto, Inos Biffi, Costante Marabelle, and Claudio Stercal. *Atlante storico della cultura medievale in Occidente*. Milan: Jaca Book, 2007.

Duby, Georges. *The Age of the Cathedrals: Art and Society, 980–1420*. Translated by Eleanor Levieux and Barbara Thompson. Chicago, IL: University of Chicago Press, 1981.

Landes, David S. *Revolution in Time: Clocks and the Making of the Modern World*. Cambridge, MA and London: The Belknap Press of Harvard University Press, 1983.

Le Goff, Jacques. *Medieval Civilization 400–1500*. Translated by Julia Barrow. London: Blackwell Publishing, 1991.

Recht, Ronald. *Believing and Seeing: The Art of Gothic Cathedrals*. Translated by Mary Whittall. Cambridge University Press, 2010.

Southern, Richard William. *The Making of the Middle Ages*. New Haven, CT: Yale University Press, 1953.

THE TIME OF THE RENAISSANCE

Berenson, Bernard. *Italian Pictures of the Renaissance*. London: Phaidon Press, 1968.

Braunstein, Philippe, and Robert Delort. *Venise, portrait historique d'une cité*. Paris: Éditions du Seuil, 1971.

Chastel, André. *Italian Art*. New York, NY: Harper & Row, 1963.

De Conihout, Isabelle, Fritsch, Julia, Jan Jaap L. Haspels, et al. *Ces curieux navires: trois automates de la Renaissance*. Paris: Réunion des Musées Nationaux, 1999.

Evans, Robert Weston. *Rudolf II and his World: A Study in Intellectual History. 1576-1612*. Oxford University Press, 1973.

Impey, Oliver, and Arthur MacGregor, eds. *The Origins of Museums: The Cabinet of Curiosities in Sixteenth- and Seventeenth-Century Europe*. Oxford: Clarendon Press, 1985.

Panofsky, Erwin. *The Life and Art of Albrecht Dürer*. Princeton, NJ: Princeton University Press, 1943.

Pomian, Krzysztof. *Collectionneurs, amateurs et curieux, Paris-Venise, XVI-XVIIIᵉ siècle*. Paris: Gallimard, 1987.

THE TIME OF THE GRAND SIÈCLE

Cole, Charles Woolsey. *Colbert and a Century of French Mercantilism*. New York, NY: Columbia University Press, 1939.

Peyre, Henri. *Qu'est-ce que le classicisme?* Paris: Nizet, 1983.

Teyssèdre, Bernard. *L'Art français au siècle de Louis XIV*. Paris: Le Livre de Poche, 1967.

Weigert, Roger-Armand. *Le Style Louis XIV*. Paris: Larousse, 1941.

THE TIME OF THE ENLIGHTENMENT

Arasse, Daniel. *Histoires de peintures*. Paris: Éditions Denoël, 2004.

Chaunu, Pierre. *La Civilisation de l'Europe des Lumières*, Paris: Arthaud, 1971.

Kimball, Fiske. *The Creation of the Rococo*. Philadelphia, PA: Philadelphia Museum of Art, 1943.

Mauzi, Robert. *L'Idée de bonheur dans la littérature et la pensée françaises au xviiiᵉ siècle*. Paris: Albin Michel, 1994.

Mortier, Roland, and Hervé Hasquin. *Étude sur le XVIIIᵉ siècle. Rocaille. Rococo*. Brussels: Éditions de l'Université de Bruxelles, 1996.

Pomeau, René. *L'Europe des Lumières. Cosmopolitisme et unité européenne au XVIIIᵉ siècle*. Paris: Hachette, 1995.

Roche, Daniel. *The Culture of Clothing: Dress and Fashion in the Ancien Régime*. Translated by Jean Birrell. Cambridge University Press, 1996.

Salmon, Xavier, ed. *Dansez, embrassez qui vous voudrez: fêtes et plaisirs d'amour au siècle de Madame de Pompadour*. Lens: Louvre-Lens, 2015. Published in conjunction with the exhibition at the Louvre-Lens, Lens.

Salmon, Xavier, ed. *Madame de Pompadour et les arts*. Paris: Réunion des Musées Nationaux, 2002.

THE TIME OF MODERNITY

Antal, Frederick. *Classicism and Romanticism, with Other Studies in Art History*. London: Routledge & Kegan Paul, 1966.

Barbey d'Aurevilly, Jules. *Dandyism*. Translated by Douglas Ainslee. Preface by Quentin Crisp. New York, NY: PAJ Publications, 2001.

Brion, Marcel. *Art of the Romantic Era*. London: Thames & Hudson, 1966.

Chenoune, Farid. *A History of Men's Fashion*. Translated by Deke Dusinberre. Paris: Flammarion, 1993.

Honour, Hugh. *Neo-Classicism. Style and Civilization*. Harmondsworth: Pelican, 1968.

Pariset, François-Georges. *L'Art néo-classique*. Paris: Presses Universitaires de France, 1974.

THE TIME OF INDUSTRY AND ENTERPRISE

L'Art en France sous le Second Empire. Paris: Réunion des Musées Nationaux, 1979. Published in conjunction with the exhibition at the Grand Palais, Paris.

Barjot, Dominique, ed. *Les Entrepreneurs du Second Empire*. Paris: Presses de l'Université Paris-Sorbonne, 2003.

Giedion, Sigfried. *Mechanization Takes Command: A Contribution to Anonymous History*. Oxford University Press, 1948.

Rosen, Charles, and Henir Zerner. *Romanticism and Realism: the Mythology of Nineteenth-Century Art*. New York, NY: Viking Press, 1984.

Yon, Jean-Claude. *Le Second Empire: politique, société, culture*. Paris: Armand Colin, 2004.

THE TIME OF THE AVANT-GARDES

Exposition internationale des Arts décoratifs industriels modernes. 1925. Rapport général. Vols. I to XII. Paris: Larousse, 1925.

Brion-Guerry, Liliane, ed. *L'Année 1913: les formes esthétiques de l'œuvre d'art à la veille de la Première Guerre mondiale*. 3 vols. Paris: Klincksieck, 1971-1973.

Brunhammer, Yvonne, and Suzanne Tise. *The Decorative Arts in France: 1900–1942*, New York, NY: Rizzoli, 1990.

Frampton, Kenneth. *Modern Architecture: A Critical History*. London: Thames & Hudson, 1980.

Veronesi, Giulia, and Lara-Vinca Masini. *Stile 1925. Ascesa e caduta delle Arts Déco*. Florence: Vallecchi, 1966.

TIME FOR ALL

Codognato, Attilia, ed. *PopArt: evoluzione di una generazione*. Milan: Electa Editrice, 1980.

Flamand, Brigitte, ed. *Le design: essais sur des théories et des pratiques*. Paris: Institut Français de la Mode / Éditions du Regard, 2006.

Francis, Mark, ed. *Les années pop, 1956-1968*. Paris: Centre Pompidou, 2001. Published in conjunction with the exhibition at the Centre National d'Art et de Culture Georges Pompidou, Paris.

Laurent, Stéphane. *Chronologie du design*. Paris: Flammarion, 1999.

Popper, Frank. *Art–Action and Participation*. New York, NY: New York University Press, 1975.

Reiss. Julie H. *From Margin to Center: The Spaces of Installation Art*. Boston, MA: MIT Press, 1999.

TIME AND BEYOND

Chilvers, Ian, and John Glaves-Smith. *A Dictionary of Modern and Contemporary Art*. 3rd online edition. Oxford University Press, 2016.

Fischer, Hervé. *L'avenir de l'art*. Montreal: VLB Éditeur, 2007.

Heinich, Nathalie. *Le Paradigme de l'art contemporain: Structures d'une révolution artistique*. Paris: Gallimard, 2014.

Le Thorel-Daviot, Pascale. *Nouveau dictionnaire des artistes contemporains*. Paris: Larousse, 2010.

Millet, Catherine. *Contemporary Art in France*. Paris: Flammarion, 2006.

TEXTS BY DOMINIQUE FLÉCHON

Augarde, Jean-Dominique. *Les Ouvriers du temps*. Geneva: Antiquorum, 1996.

Bailly, Christian, and Sharon Bailly. *Automata: The Golden Age, 1848–1914*. New York, NY: Sotheby Parke Bernet Publications, 1988.

Bach, Henri, Jean-Pierre Rieb, and Robert Wilhelm. *Les Trois Horloges astronomiques de la cathédrale de Strasbourg*. Strasbourg: Ronald Hirle, 1992.

Defossez, Léopold. *Les Savants du XVIIᵉ siècle et la mesure du temps*. Lausanne: Journal suisse d'horlogerie et de bijouterie, 1946.

Dohrn-van Rossum, Gerhard. *History of the Hour: Clocks and Modern Temporal Orders*. Translated by Thomas Dunlap. Chicago, IL: University of Chicago Press, 1996.

Diderot et d'Alembert. *Encyclopédie ou Dictionnaire raisonné, des arts et des métiers*. Paris: 1751–1760.

Fléchon, Dominique. *The Mastery of Time*. Paris: Flammarion–Fondation de la Haute Horlogerie, 2011.

Fléchon, Dominique. "La Copie: âge d'or et décadence." *Geneva: Europa Star Première*, no. 2 (vol. 18), 2016.

Fléchon, Dominique, and Chantal Fléchon. "La Pendule au Nègre." *Bulletin de l'Association Nationale des Collectioneurs et Amateurs d'Horlogerie Ancienne*, no. 63, 1992.

Fléchon, Dominique, and Grégory Gardinetti. *Horology: A Child of Astronomy*. La Croix-sur-Lutry: Watchprint.com, 2015.

Tardy, Henri Lengelle. *French Clocks: The World Over*. Paris: Tardy, 1981.

Ungerer, Alfred. *Les Horloges astronomiques et monumentales les plus remarquables de l'Antiquité à nos jours*. Strasbourg: published by the author, 1931.

INDEX OF PEOPLE AND COMPANIES

INDEX OF TIMEPIECES

PHOTOGRAPHIC CREDITS

Fig. 2.